# THIS BOY WE MADE

# THIS BOY
# WE MADE

A Memoir of Motherhood, Genetics,
and Facing the Unknown

# TAYLOR HARRIS

Catapult  New York

This book is a memoir. It reflects the author's recollections of experiences over time. Some names and identifying details have been changed to protect the privacy of individuals.

ISBN: 978-1-948226-84-4

*Jacket design by Nicole Caputo*
*Book design by Jordan Koluch*

Library of Congress Control Number: 2021936350

Catapult
1140 Broadway, Suite 704
New York, NY 10001

Printed in the United States of America

10 9 8 7 6 5 4 3 2 1

To Eliot, Tophs, and Juliet—
I don't know why I get to be yours.

Thank you, God, for creating us. Instead of putting us on pages and making us a show, you made us come to life.

—Tophs's bedtime prayer

# THIS BOY WE MADE

I stand, holding him in a pool. His knees pulled toward his slick, brown chest in a frog pose, his feet resting against my belly, as though he could push off and slip into backstroke. I look away, find the horizon, that seam between earth and space. Without meaning to, I've traded caution for wonder and lost my grip on his wrists.

There he is, below, sitting alone at the bottom of the pool. I sink beneath in one silent motion. Is he smiling, or are his lips only parted? He's okay, it seems, but who will ever forget that I let him go?

This dream only comes once at night. But pieces of it, appearing as still shots—a mother with long, dark hair; a cross-legged boy underwater—capture my mind throughout the day, inviting me to assign meaning, give the dream's airy form depth.

Guilt. Maybe this dream is about a mother's guilt. What did I do—or not do?

Maybe it was the missed feeding in the hospital before his circumcision. I'd slept so long, and the doctor whisked him away that morning *before I could hold his loose lips, which never did latch, to my breast. They gave him sugar water after the procedure, and he slept and slept.*

*Twenty-two months later, we would rush him to the hospital for more sugar water, this time by a slow drip into his veins.*

*But what if my dream is just about the boy? About this gorgeous boy sitting, wide eyes open, underwater; not flailing, not failing, not drowning, just being? If that is true, then who is this boy, and what does he need? Can I give it? Imagine—maybe his mother never dropped him at all. Maybe, one way or another, the boy would have wound up sitting on the smooth bottom of the pool, looking straight ahead.*

This is the life we have, in skin and bones, living in between.

—KATE BOWLER

Paul found him that morning. Our twenty two month old boy, staring and still, awake without a sound. A twenty pound toddler in blue pajamas, lying across the only thing we allowed in his crib—a taut cotton sheet.

Tophs hadn't smiled to reveal the dimple planted deep on his left cheek or hopped up on his short, thick feet to call for me. Even though he was almost two, he didn't always call me "Mommy" or Paul "Daddy." Sometimes he switched our names around or stole Paul's pet name for me. "Baaaaaabe! Baaaaaabe!" The adult word in Tophs's raspy baby voice never grew old.

He called his three-year-old sister, Eliot, "babe" too. They shared a room across the hall and often awoke together, but that morning, Eliot got up, ready to eat breakfast, and Tophs barely roused.

Paul handed him over to me in our bedroom. "He didn't cry or anything. He was just up."

I didn't usually put Tophs in our bed. Not only did I cherish my own space, but as a newborn, he'd rolled off my side of the bed one morning after I'd dozed off. Even though I'd called the doctor immediately and he'd stopped crying within a minute, I worried I'd fractured his skull or jilted his brain just enough to cause a small but dangerous bleed.

Now he was much bigger, so I folded Tophs, who seemed to store all body fat in his cheeks, into my arms, then into bed, thankful for an extra hour of sleep. With Eliot's preschool on spring break and Paul teaching on Grounds, I had a full day ahead of playing tennis with foam balls in the hallway of our University of Virginia faculty apartment, a glorified dormitory suite with cinderblock walls, or listening to music on the desktop while the kids stomped on alphabet squares. If the weather turned warm, we might walk through the gardens where students grew cantaloupes and lettuce, spices and sunflowers, and left extras at our door. No Starbucks drive-thru existed back then, so my daily trip out for a latte required me to load the kids into the van, drive fifteen minutes, unload them, strap them into a heavy double stroller, then guide that clunky monster through the door, sweat pooling under my pits, while a nice old man in classic walking shorts and loafers remarked, "Well, you certainly have your hands full, don't you?" As a mother of two, just grabbing a coffee took straight-up balls.

I don't know who or what woke us from that morning nap—was it Eliot, with her curly Afro and sparkly tutu, running down the long hallway, or Paul, pulling on slacks for work? I do know Tophs reached for his blue kid-sized CamelBak and sucked down water like he'd been waiting days for a drink. As he lay on his back, his cotton pajama shirt quivered with each pump of his heart. I placed my hand over his chest. The beats too strong, too quick. But maybe it was nothing. Maybe it was the old me, noticing.

I carried Tophs into our small kitchen, seating him at the kiddie wooden table he and Eliot shared. He usually loved diced peaches in juice or what he and his big sister called "blue shoo shoo": granola cereal in a blue box from Trader Joe's. Instead, he turned his head away from anything I put in front of him, except for that water bottle. He drank and drank.

If I couldn't feed my child, I could at least change his diaper. I moved him to our family room with its airplane-aisle-thin carpet, only a slight upgrade from the student rooms above us. When Tophs was learning to sit up, I'd surrounded him with pillows or a Boppy cushion, because when he fell, as he often did with a body that was near the fifth percentile for height and weight and a head that measured near the eightieth, he basically hit concrete. It was on that hard floor I placed him while I opened the faux-leather ottoman to grab a diaper and wipes. Before I could finish, before I could pull each strap forward from the back and fasten them to the front, before I could tug his blue pajama pants up toward his waist, he had fallen back asleep. Our son with the beautiful face, the one who loved to clap in circles around the apartment or doctor's office or sidewalk, stretched out and still between us.

A picture, stored on our computer, shows Tophs rolled over on his left side. You can only see the back of his head, then his legs, slightly bent, and it's only haunting if you were there, if you know he's not just another kid nodding off in the corner. I must have taken the photo as proof, to show the doctor in case this turned out to be nothing. *See? I had good reason to be concerned*, I'd say. She'd nod in agreement, maybe we'd share a laugh: *Kids are such mysteries, aren't they?*

If Tophs was merely tired or recovering from a recent stomach virus—if this was no big deal but I overreacted and called the doctor—then I'd be the mother I said I'd never become: a mother ruled by fear, incapable of parsing fact from myth. Forget all the times I'd properly cared for Eliot, when I'd found a rash the doctor wanted to see or guessed right about an ear infection. Forget the fact that no parent gets it right every time. When I have to make a quick parenting decision, I put my motherhood on trial. I remember the slippery pieces of evidence that probably shouldn't even be reviewed, like the face of a white male doctor who'd questioned my decision to give Eliot Tylenol for a fever under 102 degrees. "Fever is the body's natural response," he'd said, seemingly annoyed. Then, "Where did you say you live again?" As though living on the wrong side of the county line would explain my incompetence. The photo of Tophs would guard me from the shame I'd felt with that doctor. So would Paul's opinion.

"This isn't normal," I told him, looking down at Tophs. "I think I should call." My offering a litmus test, Paul's chance to tell me to *calm down* but in kinder words. (We'd banned *calm down* early in our marriage.) *Let's give it some time*, he might say. Paul was the steady one in our marriage with the reliable academic job, who still kept an Icy Hot container full of silver dollars he'd saved up as a kid in an old gym bag under the bed. He routinely shaved his head every few days and wore a white button-down shirt with slacks to work. (Black professors aren't afforded the luxury of wearing jeans or sneakers to lecture.) I could count on Paul to avoid excess, unless it was a bowl of cereal near midnight, and to always think before responding, unless he heard a gospel chord on the organ. It's no coincidence that I fell in love with a counselor. I found, still find, my footing in his measuredness.

We'd met on the green Charlottesville trolley twelve years before, his face not unlike our son's now—full, brown cheeks and black eyelashes that swept down before curling, scooping me up right along with them. He already knew my name, had seen me around Thomas Jefferson's Grounds. Thankfully, he wore a nametag. The youngest son of a Harlem preacher, he'd been named after the apostle.

A few weeks later, we bumped into each other near the sheet cake at a celebration for Black students. I was nineteen, flirtatious, and before I thought too much of the words, they flew out of my mouth: "Wanna get married sometime?" He was twenty-two and flirtatious, and before he thought too much of the answer, it spilled from his lips: "I was just thinking the same thing."

The boy was an old soul. He invited me over to his graduate assistant apartment, a couple of rooms at the bottom of a freshman dorm, for grilled cheese fresh off his George Foreman. A scripture typed in cursive and framed in cheap gold sat on his bookshelf. I hated the gaudy style but loved the words: "Trust in the Lord with all your heart, and lean not on your own understanding. In all your ways, acknowledge Him, and He will direct your path."

This boy was safe. Gentle. We watched *SportsCenter* in the dark, my head on his lap, and he didn't make a move. I thought of all the mediocre white boys I'd crushed on growing up, many of whom never even saw me. Maybe those days were over.

If Paul thought a trip to the doctor could wait, I'd believe him. Although this time it wasn't Eliot's nagging cough or Tophs's acid reflux that caught my attention. My boy, who was barely hanging on to the growth chart with one hand, lay heavy as a rock on the floor.

"What do you think?" I tried to read the way Paul leaned slightly forward, how his hands touched together in the center, whether his eyebrows looked weighted and serious or light with thought.

"I trust your decision, babe," he said, and often says. It's not a bait and switch. It's everything I should want to hear. My spouse respecting my knowledge, honoring the time I've spent raising our children as a stay-at-home mom while he worked as a professor by day and attended seminary on the weekends. But his words also emphasized that this was *my* decision. The sun would rise and set with me. I had the length of the horizon to fail.

I stifled my fear of being labeled a mother who exaggerates long enough to tell the receptionist all I'd seen: Lethargy. Racing heart. No food. Lots of water. No fever.

"We can see you at 9:30."

This is where motherhood divided into Before and After.

In the Before, I pumped breast milk, drove a minivan, and blogged about it. I returned to my alma mater, the University of

Virginia, as a grown woman, and learned to push my kids' double stroller past the campus buses without feeling too old and washed out. I drank my way to a Starbucks gold card and chose lattes over new clothes every month. With just four hours of sleep and a mocha in hand, I could do anything. Charlottesville, a city known for its beauty and history, started to feel like home, not just the college town I was introduced to as a skinny eighteen-year-old from Ohio.

Before, I tried to keep Tophs on the growth chart by feeding him good fats: avocados, olive oil, butter-drenched everything. "Roll his peas in butter," Dr. Quillian, his pediatrician, had said. "Do the opposite of what we've learned as adults." We puzzled over his lack of growth, that he'd weighed two pounds less than his big sister at birth. But with those round cheeks and feet so cute in tiny New Balances, with his rhythmic clapping and alert, curious eyes, no one truly worried.

In the Before, I wrote a column about raising toddlers in a college dorm where sleep-training Tophs caused a student to knock on our door and ask if we could "keep the noise down." "Oh, you mean the *baby*?!" we yelled back. I walked the kids down to the dining hall for Belgian waffles and pointed to the trolley where Mommy and Daddy first met.

Before included training for a ten-miler because I was turning thirty and fighting the ghost of my undergrad self, who showed so much promise and would take over the world by thirty-five. Life was neither simple nor without grief Before, but I recognized its parts. I knew what was hard and what wasn't. Being a Black mother in a city, and country, built for whites was hard. So was living with an anxiety disorder. These were heavy yet familiar crosses to bear.

I knew their weight, knew where the wood notched. They were, I thought, enough.

*After* came three days after I crossed the finish line of that ten-miler and two days after my thirtieth birthday. In the After, Tophs stared at nothing, those eyes empty—a world fallen flat—as a nurse with thick glasses and mousy hair checked his pulse, then whispered, "It's fast."

Dr. Quillian didn't work Tuesdays, so Tophs saw another doctor on the team we'd met. Dr. Marcus Potter was African American, young, and warm. She was the kind of mom I wanted to be friends with and the kind of professional I wanted my Black children to see.

Tophs sat on the crinkly paper stretched over the table as she shone a light into his eyes and listened to his chest. She lowered him back, palpated his stomach, then pulled him up to sitting. He still exhibited some strength, she noted. He didn't let his head flop back. Yet neither the look on her face—part curiosity, part concern—nor her questions reassured me.

"Does he normally look like this?"

I knew what she meant—his eyes wide and vacant.

"Is there any chance he got into medicine or something poisonous?" She looked at me, her straight brown bob framing her face, but then turned back to Tophs.

I mentally scanned the previous day. This answer would normally be an easy no, but a memory broke through and startled me with its potential for guilt: the day before, Paul had stayed home with the kids while I went out, and he'd mentioned falling asleep on the floor while they played. Even at three, Eliot acted like the mature, older sibling, so I hadn't worried. Paul didn't drink coffee, and unplanned power naps got him through long days. But what if this was Paul's fault? What if, between seminary and teaching, he'd exhausted himself and dropped the ball? It felt like betrayal, but I told her the story. If Tophs had swallowed Windex or Tylenol, she needed to know.

She listened but didn't seem alarmed. I asked about his brain. What if he were bleeding somewhere? Should we rush him in for a CT scan? But Dr. Marcus Potter wasn't particularly worried about internal bleeding either.

The night before, Tophs had bit me hard on my shoulder in the buffet line at the dining hall, out of nowhere, and I'd dug my thumb into him, near his collarbone, forcing him to let go. I'd been angry in the moment, surprised by the pain. What if I'd punctured something? Why hadn't I just endured the bite? What if I'd put something in motion that would lead to his slow, labored death? I told Dr. Marcus Potter about the uncharacteristic bite but not my reaction. I'd been willing to tell on my husband, even my son, but not on myself.

"If he doesn't perk up by this afternoon, why don't you give us a call and bring him back in for bloodwork? Does that sound good? Are you comfortable with that plan?" I noticed how much she wanted to put me at ease. I would not be the pushy mother accused of false alarm, so *that sounds good.*

I remember maneuvering our stroller, standing by our van, and answering my phone, something I rarely did as an introvert, because it was Paul on the other end. But I don't remember having Eliot with me. I only know she was there because the doctor's notes capture her presence: "Mom and sister" the record reads. Did she, a quiet observer with a strong memory, trap her brother's strangely still body in her mind that morning? Did she notice the nurse's quick steps, the doctor's uncertain face—or how the lack of an answer was not the same as saying "Everything will be okay"?

I worry that even when she seems content, when she's playing school or reading a book, Eliot might sense this erasure—that as the more medically stable, independent firstborn, she'll be haunted by moments when her mother could only see the child who more often fell outside the margins.

"Are you still there?" Paul asked.

"We just left. I'm getting them into the van." He deserved a full update, but I couldn't talk and keep the kids safe in the parking lot.

"Okay, don't leave. They just called me. They're trying to catch you. They want to do bloodwork *now*."

Dr. Marcus Potter, a mother of young children, couldn't shake the feeling that something wasn't right. She met me inside the third-floor office. "If we do the bloodwork now, we can have results by the afternoon," she said. "I just don't feel right about sending you home."

In the After, the same nurse who took his pulse drew blood from the crook of Tophs's arm. He didn't flinch or squirm or whine. Later she'd tell me how much that scared her. Me too. It's rarely Tophs thrashing about or crying that chills me; it's the slow and heavy silence.

When we left the office for good, I didn't yet know I was in the After, so I carried over routines from Before: I stopped at the Route 29 Starbucks for caffeine with Tophs slumped over my shoulder. Eliot, always cautious in public, must have walked closely behind me. I ordered a morning bun, and Tophs picked his head up off my shoulder long enough to eat half, the first bites he'd taken all day.

He was sleeping again, the back of his head cradled in my left arm, when Dr. Marcus Potter called a few hours later. "Mrs. Harris, we got Christopher's bloodwork back, and the results are concerning. I'm not even sure they're accurate."

Not accurate? What did that even mean?

"You all live close to the hospital, right? I want you to take him to the ER now."

I grabbed the diapers and water bottles, the stroller and shoes, my purse and my kids, all without a scream or a curse, in under five minutes. I have lived much of my life this way—detached but efficient under real pressure, a panicked mess when no real threat exists. I am built for fight or flight. My brain, a barely balanced sprinter in the starting block of my body, craves permission—the sound of a blank shot through the air—to run at full speed. Sometimes my brain gets it right. More often, the sound was merely the click of spikes in the next lane, a kid jumping down rows of metal bleachers, a volunteer slamming the concession stand door shut.

As I stepped outside, Paul was running up the ramp toward me. Dr. Marcus Potter had called him at work, and he'd caught the campus bus home. My self-assured and practical Paul, who'd bought a pair of Rockports in his twenties because they were comfortable, showed up without delay or question. He ran, signaling how serious this situation must be, and I saw his swift movements as validation. For once, his angst matched, maybe surpassed, mine. In this strange and tilted world, panic emerged as the new normal.

We drove five minutes to the University of Virginia Medical Center, and, for the first time in my life, someone waited for us at the front. "Christopher Harris?" asked a man in scrubs. Only doctors and new teachers call Tophs by his real name.

I was ready to follow him, with Tophs in my arms, when an employee behind the registration desk stopped us. He did not offer us the Black person head nod and seemed instantly irritated by our presence. I wanted to honor his request for our address and phone numbers, our birthdays and insurance information. Sure, I'm a people pleaser. But I also can't ignore the deep divide in Charlottesville. Mostly whites are the haves—the tenured professors, surgeons, bankers, and entrepreneurs—and it's not uncommon to see Blacks in service roles. Everything in me wanted to please this brother and avoid trampling on his personhood. Yet, with his head cocked to the side as he typed, his voice monotonous, it was clear how little he cared about our son's need for immediate help.

Finally, the man who'd greeted us spoke up: "If one of you wants to finish up here and the other bring him on back . . ."

"I'm almost finished," Mr. Registration snapped, and I wanted to squeeze his neck until his mouth opened up wide and the pit of his stomach felt as fiery and desperate as mine. But when I think of that moment now, I'm not sure if I'm mad at a Black stranger for lacking empathy or pissed at myself for being the kind of mother who would let her kid suffer while she acquiesced. A mother whose desire to appear normal, to seem rational, to be liked, weakened her ability to care for her son.

The man in scrubs led us through double doors to a room on the left side of the pediatric ER, across from the nurses station. An old curtain I was scared to touch or let Eliot sit against separated us from a patient on the other side. As though moving in double time, a team in scrubs and white coats appeared and began assessing Tophs. I couldn't leave the room, but as Eliot's huge eyes took it all in, I worried that watching her brother being acted upon by strangers might scar her. I worried she was like me, quietly collecting threats, clutching them tight in her hands, until the day she'd look down and panic, unable to separate her own hands from the fear they held. Though she likely sat on Paul's lap, in my mind, she's crouched in the corner near the stained curtain with her pink junior backpack, wanting to appear as small as possible while observing every single move.

Tophs, awake but dazed, sat in a huge white bed while they poked his finger, started an IV, and drew blood.

"Why isn't he seizing?" someone yelled.

*I* never heard that question. Paul had to tell me later. How was I so swallowed by the scene that I missed it? Our son should have been seizing. That's what can happen when your blood glucose drops to 27mg/dL. The low end of normal is 70mg/dL. That's why Dr. Marcus Potter wasn't sure if the results were correct.

We walked the medical team through Tophs's dinner the previous night—half a slice of pizza and vanilla soft-serve from the dining hall—and how we didn't think he'd swallowed poison even though Paul had napped. We mentioned his recent stomach virus. When I told them that I'd fed him half a Starbucks morning bun after his appointment, the attending doctor popped her head up from his bedside. "Good mommy!" she said. What does it mean that the praise of this woman made me feel like a straight-A student and the arm of God? I'd met my boy's need, even if I had backed into it through the tired fog of motherhood. I still can't bring myself to imagine what might have happened if I had gotten more sleep the night before, if Starbucks hadn't been my second home.

Without food, how long does a boy with a glucose level of twenty-seven have? Would a coma have come next?

As Tophs, with dextrose running through his veins, devoured two ice pops and perked up, the staff seemed encouraged, their movements slowed. He would stay overnight for more tests, but the crisis had ended.

We waited there, in the After, relieved and numb, still mostly in the dark as to why a little boy's body could come crashing down on itself.

Here's the thing about After: it can stay forever.

2

The room on the pediatric floor of the hospital held a crib with heavy white gates on either side and an armchair I wouldn't have converted into a bed, even if I'd known how. Hospitals have always been a great source of mystery and fear for me. They are home to blood and germs, yet healing and mending too. Growing up, I saw them as magical fortresses. If my throat were to swell from an anaphylactic reaction, I only had to make it to a hospital to be spared. If a vessel in my brain bulged and leaked, I just needed to cross the ER's threshold to be saved. Doctors did what no other humans could do. They were death's antidote.

I was five, sitting in the front seat of our family's bronze-colored van with velvety curtains as Mom drove down Broad Street in Columbus, Ohio, past towering trees and a large brick synagogue.

I don't know why the conversation started, but I mentioned the death of an elderly relative. It was likely my great-aunt Garnett, my paternal grandmother's aunt, who had been friends with Langston Hughes in her younger years. To me, she was a light-brown, wrinkled woman mostly confined to a bed that cranked up and down with the push of a button. She had helped raise my grandmother and lived in a room in Grandma's house, and everything I experienced during visits—from Aunt Garnett's white hair to the house's green carpet to the scent of rubbing alcohol or medicine hovering over the smell of baked chicken or green beans—signaled death to my young brain. I had attended Aunt Garnett's funeral and interment, my cousins and I bouncing in the backseat of the van as the tires rolled over the cemetery's gravel path. I wore a dress and probably folded-down white socks with frills. The cemetery proved a scary place, but we were young, and Aunt Garnett was there because she was old.

As Mom drove, I reflected on the fact that old people—a group of people *born* scaly with thin gray hair and bones (what a poor lot!)—died. It's what they did. What happened to *them*.

"Taylor, we all die sometime," Mom said. I can see her soft brown hair, curled with hot rollers each morning but falling along her face in wisps anyway, her fair forearms that barely tanned enough in the summer to leave a watch-shaped mark on her wrist. Mom's voice is smooth as the middle of sliced almonds in my memories, her neck sweet with the smell of lavender or vanilla, so I know she meant no harm. The mother who feeds you cookies after morning kindergarten and flies a Snoopy kite with you in the park never means to topple your world, send you falling off the flat sides you'd constructed. "I don't want to die!" I wailed, and I don't know if it was her touch, or her words "It won't happen right now," or only time that made me stop.

Now that I have my own children, I've realized not every child responds with the same bitter shock as I did that day. Something about death's wholeness—death's size and movement, its lack of boundaries—struck a part of me already prone to fear and despair.

When Dr. Marcus Potter called my cell phone at the hospital, I was still under some naïve impressions—not that death comes only to old people but that doctors have more answers than questions, and hospitals, while imperfect, are brick-and-mortar sites of healing.

"How are you?"

I stared at the devices and wires hooked to the wall behind Tophs's bed. "He's getting dextrose through the IV and looking much better."

"I mean *mentally* how are you doing? This is a lot."

Could I have felt the weight of her question if I'd wanted? But I was running on adrenaline fumes, acting as though I could throw my anxiety disorder overboard like excess cargo whenever one of my children needed me. So my answer was *I am fine, my boy is fine, we are all fine.* I still didn't know how abnormal Tophs's levels actually were, that it wasn't just about blood sugar but also pH levels and the body's chain reactions and all sorts of numbers on his metabolic panel flagged as too high or low.

I thanked her for calling me back into the office, for not being too proud to follow her hunch. She'd helped us through this random storm. I saved her number; she said I could call anytime. I appreciated her tenderness, but I didn't want her to invest too much energy in caring for my mental state, because Tophs would go home the next day. Strange things happened that didn't alter a person's trajectory. Growing up, I'd heard stories about a tic that put my oldest sister in the hospital as a baby but then disappeared. And how my middle sister's face became paralyzed on one side during a bad case of chicken pox before her feeling fully returned. One day I would tell the story of the morning Tophs's body went eerily limp, then regained strength with an IV and ice pop. This was no big deal in the long run, because this was almost over, and soon we'd return home to the landscape of Before.

In the meantime, I received my first assignment from hospital staff: collecting a urine sample from Tophs, because no one had secured one in the ER. Apparently, because his penis had formed in my womb, I held the maternal powers to direct his wayward stream. A nurse showed me the sterilized bag, how I could tape it around his scrotum before replacing his diaper. I laid Tophs on his back, the crib gate lifted, and did my best to trap his penis, but when the nurse came back, she seemed disappointed. No, she said. I hadn't done it right. I stayed next to Tophs but backed away in my mind to let her try. Satisfied with her taping job, she left the room, only to return a while later to find his diaper soaked with urine, the bag empty. Call me petty, but I loved to see it. Another nurse, known on the floor for her pee-trapping ways, arrived and eventually succeeded.

I held Tophs all night in the armchair; he wouldn't have any of that cage-like crib, and after a day of unfamiliar people prodding him, who could blame him? Paul had taken Eliot home for the night, and I was uncomfortable in that chair yet content being a simple but good mother, holder of soft limbs, smoother of curls, and kisser of cheeks.

The room's darkness broke again and again throughout the night as a nurse checked his vitals. I fell in and out of sleep, my arms aching under the load of my boy. I'd grown used to seeing the purple-and-white hospital glucometer every hour or so. An alcohol swab, a quick prick of Tophs's skin, then a few seconds' countdown until a digital number appeared. I would eye the number, usually within normal limits, and then let my head fall back, assured the nurse and dextrose were both doing their jobs.

During one of those past-midnight checks, when the world outside was closed but the monitors inside beeped, I woke up to see 400 on the glucometer screen. "Let me call the doctor and see if they want us to stop the dextrose," the nurse said calmly. My eyes followed her across the room to where she made a call, like a shadow of a person I'd imagined.

Even today, I want to scream, "Four hundred?! Rip out the IV!" but, instead, I nodded off again until the nurse got permission to change the dosage. I never mentioned that number to any of the doctors at the hospital or Tophs's regular pediatrician. It seemed part of a dream sequence I was glad to see end. There's a twilight-zone aura to a hospital at night—an inner world of neon overhead lights and monitors running on energy that the sleepy world outside has turned off. Maybe I'd made it all up, the night-shift nurse and her quick phone call merely ghosts of my disoriented mind.

I have spent a lifetime striving to ignore the shapes and sounds of night. As I child, I told myself that the train I heard through my bedroom window didn't carry monsters, elevator doors didn't stay closed forever, and darkness didn't always usher in death.

One evening I stood close to my mom in Drug Emporium, where we purchased things called toiletries that Mom said were taxable. When the bill was high, we blamed rubbing alcohol or face wash. While I wasn't yet in grade school, I was old enough to feel squeamish when Mom had to write a check, hoping it didn't bounce, a word that sounded fun but I sensed brought shame. That evening, as she scanned a shelf for an item on the list she wrote in looped cursive, the lights dimmed to warn us the store would soon close. Panic has no name when you're that young, but the walls of my brain collapsed inward, and I was certain we would be stuck in the store with no way out.

"Mommy, Mommy!" I pulled on her purse or pant leg. "We have to go! Now!"

"Taz, honey, it's okay. We aren't locked in. We'll go check out and they'll open the doors for us." Mom talked as though she were reading a textbook, and the evenness often soothed me, but this time I wouldn't rest until the air outside touched my face.

If I were an artist, I'd paint the picture of that memory on a broad swath of canvas, call it "Panic in Aisle 4." I'd paint a round brown girl with a forest-green-and-fuchsia coat, turquoise Reebok sneakers, a mother's soft and feathered 1980s hairstyle, a dimmed overhead light, and shelves filled with Jergens lotion and Oil of Olay.

Maybe I'd paint a whole series, me in sepia, brushing up against the orange fire pit of anxiety. Again as an older child, a teenager, then as an adult, panicked—on airplanes, in math class, under the streetlights of Madrid, in the recovery room of a hospital as doctors puzzled over my vital signs. I'd create an installation for every night in my life when I hoped the men I saw like trees, walking, were just that—trees. My life makes the most sense when, as dawn breaks, I discover the only limbs I feared were those wrapped in bark.

Paul returned with Eliot and coffee the next morning, and I wanted to apologize to other parents as my healthy kids tore through the hallways and bounced around the playroom. The only evidence of the previous day's ordeal was a stiff board wrapped around Tophs's left arm in yellow gauze, a cotton ball taped over an injection site on his right arm, and two hospital bracelets around his ankle. Oh, and his pants were missing. So he wore a navy onesie and his little gray sneakers and, in that way, looked like every other satisfied, half-dressed toddler.

Before we could go home, an entire team filed into the room, one or two people left in the hallway, unable to fit inside. No one standing in the long line of white coats said, "We don't know what happened to your son." A nervous medical student with straight red hair shakily read her notecards aloud to the crowd and, pre-sumably, us. Bless her heart, I felt more concerned for her confi-dence, her ability to pull through this, than I did for Tophs. I'm thankful for teaching hospitals, but human touch seems destined to get lost in the performance of it all.

She said Tophs had likely experienced *ketotic hypoglycemia*, a re-curring condition in which a child's blood glucose level drops after a period of fasting or illness. It's a diagnosis by exclusion, meaning the doctors' best guess when nothing else seems to make sense. A urine sample usually seals the deal, but, she briefly mentioned and moved on, something had happened to Tophs's urine sample. That liquid gold the superhero nurse had trapped in a plastic bag was gone. They'd sent blood samples to the Mayo Clinic to rule out any more serious underlying conditions, and we'd have to wait a few weeks for those results.

The team recommended Tophs never miss a meal and always eat a bedtime snack high in protein and carbs. He'd probably outgrow the episodes by eight or nine years of age. The monologue-slash-exam ended, and we, his parents, were given the floor. Several people stared adoringly at Eliot and Tophs, commenting on their cuteness, which, you know, was nice, but I was still waiting for a doctor to step in and talk to us without the awkward pauses and index cards.

"Do you all have any questions?" a doctor asked.

"You mentioned something about a urine sample," Paul said, and I knew where we were headed.

"Yes, unfortunately, we didn't get results on that."

Paul loves people but rarely feels trapped by their thoughts about him. And he's got this way of asking questions, even pointed ones, that politely pin you to the wall. A Black male, even one with a crisp goatee and blazer, must inquire in the most peculiar way, his nonverbal cues and tone alternating between calm and concern. He must not offend. He must show his spine. He must not offend.

"Didn't we collect a sample? I'm not sure I understand. What happened to it?"

I had worked so hard with those nurses to collect enough. While I'm the type to put my head down and avoid making anyone uncomfortable, I was glad Paul wasn't afraid to call out what they'd conveniently glossed over.

"Someone downstairs must have thrown the sample out" was the most we got. No effusive apology because they'd missed the window to collect sensitive data on the cause of our son's illness.

Later, I read in Tophs's record that someone had sent the urine down to the lab without orders. Hospitals are run by people, many of whom work long hours. But in these moments, Paul and I shift quickly; our thoughts go to race. If a white professor and his son had been in the same situation, would the same answer have sufficed? Even if doctors couldn't recover the sample, would they have apologized? Would they, instead, have led the conversation with what they'd lost?

When Paul told his friend Sidney, a doctor, that we were in the hospital, Sidney reminded Paul to let the staff know who he was: an alum of and professor at UVA. We could be gracious, yes, but for Black people receiving medical care, the world leaves no room for humility or deference. We knew too many stories; we'd been warned to look for disparities in treatment, but we didn't really have to be warned. We'd experienced variants of it all our lives.

Still, Tophs appeared stable and happy, and we were going home. In a last photo before discharge, he's smiling and holding Paul's iPhone. This time his shirt has somehow disappeared, but a diaper peeks out over gray stretch pants. The album cover of a gospel artist is displayed on the phone screen. Behind him, remnants of our stay adorn the hospital tray: an iced latte Paul brought, open milk cartons Tophs drank from to prove he could maintain his levels without an IV, and a new container of Play-Doh the staff said he could take with him.

We would follow up with Dr. Quillian, feed Tophs yogurt or ice cream or goldfish and smoothies every night before bed. He would, I assumed, continue to be our small boy, slow to gain weight but always dancing and making absurd faces into my phone.

As he'd entered toddlerhood, we'd exchanged Tophs's highchair for what my friend called the Chair of Death, a red seat without legs that attached to our dining room table and gave Tophs the appearance of levitating. One morning, as Tophs hung there on the side of the table, oatmeal and milk running down his shirt, we played a goofy game of improv. "Ready?" I asked him. "Whoa!" I said, like Joey from the 1990s sitcom *Blossom*. Tophs laughed for a few seconds, then looked straight ahead and gathered himself. Suddenly, he swung his face back toward me, his mouth an *O*, eyebrows raised. "Oh my gosh! Whoa!" I said again, and he stuck his tongue through the *O* of his mouth, pushing his eyebrows even higher, before breaking into a giggle, his baby teeth appearing.

I have always felt most secure in these moments as a mother. Nothing brought me more pride as a young mom than hearing Eliot laugh. And as she grew older, eliciting a laugh was a way to check in with her when she was quiet. But as Tophs's mom, humor served another purpose too. *Tophs is so funny, he has to be fine*, I told myself. No kid with such comedic timing and impeccable rhythm—he choreographed a liturgical dance to Lorde's "Royals" one afternoon—could be suffering from something serious. His brain was obviously firing and his body growing, albeit slowly. I am five-foot-two and Paul is five-foot-ten. My oldest sister finally reached five feet in college, and Paul's grandfather was a fiery five-foot-six preacher. No one expected the Harris kids to be giants.

As much as my anxiety can prod me to think the worst, after years of medication and therapy I actually spend a lot of time thinking things will be okay, not dreaming up health crises. While prayer and my faith help to still the frantic waves of my brain, so does Zoloft. There have been times I've been doing so well—drinking a latte and making my way through the aisles of Target alone, or packing a cute bento lunch for the kids, or hitting "send" on an essay submission—that I've wondered if I've mostly outgrown the fear. Maybe it died with the panic attacks of my teenage years. Maybe I've finally hit my stride and am living the life I was created to live, characterized by less paralyzing worry and more mundane *doing*.

For the first two years of Tophs's life, our family was doing the mundane pretty well. Tophs had a few health hiccups and weight checks here and there, but those were offset by moments of ridiculous joy, like when he and Eliot chanted at the dinner table while Paul beatboxed. In one of my favorite videos, Eliot shimmies in her seat and chants "U-V-A" over and over as she eats Greek yogurt, and Tophs, still too young to say the letters, sways side to side in his chair, his huge eyes staring into the camera and then over at his big sister for the next move. He was the cutest hype man we could ask for, and as he danced during meals, I allowed a quiet song to rise up in me: *Things will be okay, and it is well with my soul, because things will be okay.*

3

If something were truly wrong with my son's body, the doctors would have caught it at birth or shortly after. That's what pre-natal and newborn screenings were for. I knew a child could get a disease like cancer or diabetes or a mental illness like depression at any time. But if Tophs were missing part of a chromosome or a gene, if something were dangerously awry with his body's orig-inal design, we would know. Tophs's birth story wasn't a tale of close calls or escape. If anything, it was the story of a regular ol' midwestern Black woman giving birth in a hospital made for crunchy white folk.

Two days after I gave birth, still in my postpartum routine of scarfing down (free!) hospital Pop-Tarts without morning sick-ness to restrain me, a woman with purported supernatural milking powers arrived at my bedside. I told her, timidly, as this granola hospital's unofficial motto was *Breast is Best,* that even though my firstborn had latched *and* taken a bottle right away in the NICU, I couldn't get this baby to stay on my breast.

She didn't seem worried one bit, because lactation consultants are confident goddesses in Dansko clogs. She instructed me to hold Tophs like a football. Then she coached me to stroke his cheek and lips. She told me to place him above one breast and let him squirm his way down to my nipple like a lizard. But with each attempt, his lips felt like a limp handshake. It wasn't the baby, it's never the baby; I was failing.

Finally, she grabbed a white spoon sealed in plastic and unwrapped it, and, classy postpartum woman that I was, I could only think about Wendy's drive-thru chili. The red container filled with beans and ground beef that I used to cover with broken saltines and shredded cheese while Dad unwrapped a burger loaded with extra toppings. That man never saw a pickle slice that didn't belong in his mouth. And don't let them have a ninety-nine-cent sale on Frostys.

But there were no Frostys that day—just me, a human, trying to make actual milk. An act that was supposedly natural and only a little strange. The lactation consultant squeezed my nipple with one hand and held the spoon underneath it with the other. A few drops of fluid pooled in the center of the spoon.

"Whoa, you've got a lot of colostrum," she said.

I wanted to snatch my breast back and hide in the corner, alone with my God-given excess, but I also wanted a trophy. If my colostrum was, in fact, extraordinary, other women in the ward ought to know. I should lead workshops on Maximizing Your Colostrum.

I could not, though, teach anyone about getting their five-pound baby to latch. To be clear, Tophs weighed five pounds, fifteen and a half ounces. But that half an ounce made all the difference, bringing nurses from far and wide to see him.

"We heard there was a five-pounder!" they'd say and then look at me, as though I should give an account. I'm considered petite, but I'd gained fifty pounds with Tophs, so the fetus-to-ice-cream-sandwich ratio of my weight gain was not lost on me either. Eliot had weighed over eight pounds, so when I gained more with Tophs than I had with her, I promised everyone that I'd deliver a ten-pounder. The other forty pounds *had* to be water weight and an On-Cor family-sized placenta.

While the baby drew a small crowd, no one seemed concerned about his weight or disposition or even the way his limbs shook and shuddered at times as he lay in the bassinet. I worried about withdrawal from my antidepressant. What if Zoloft, the medicine I'd continued to take throughout my pregnancy, had already harmed him?

In the beginning of my mother's third pregnancy, she carried two of us, fraternal twins. After she lost my twin early on, her nausea only intensified, and her doctor prescribed a drug called Bendectin. After a few doses, Mom stopped taking it. Maybe a gut feeling, a hunch, or maybe she feared taking any medication during pregnancy.

One day when I was four or five, she pointed to our television screen. "That's it! That's the drug I took when I was pregnant with you." Kids missing limbs sat on the stage of a talk show. Apparently, their mothers had taken Bendectin. The drug had disappeared from grocers' shelves in 1983, the year I was born, as the manufacturer faced lawsuits. I didn't understand the details then, but from Mom's tone, the size of her eyes, I knew I had escaped something.

Zoloft, doctors told me, was generally safer for fetuses than Paxil, but no antidepressant could be labeled "safe." You had to weigh the risk of harm to the baby from the drug against the risk of harm to the baby and mother from mental illness left untreated. After hearing that I'd taken an SSRI, or serotonin reuptake inhibitor, since I was sixteen years old, none of the doctors I saw told me to wean off antidepressants altogether. The risk to mother and baby would have been too great.

Had my need to be medicated tainted this beautiful baby boy who, in the first few days of life, slept well, showed off his dimple and butt chin, and quaked? But over and over again, the medical staff cited his still-developing nervous system, so I let myself off the hook and chose to believe them. Sitting here, on the other side, I still choose to believe the nurses. I don't worry about the Zoloft, but I do wish someone had checked his blood sugar. They might have, but I don't have a record of it, so I'll always wonder if his little metabolism jumped and crashed and shook, either inside or outside the womb, or both. Perhaps some questions always hang there, unchanged, in the middle.

The lactation consultant, God bless her, wanted us to stay a few more hours before being discharged. She really wanted to see the baby latch on strong. She offered to make some rounds and come back. But we'd waited two days to see her, and she wasn't going to ruin our plans to go home and never sleep again. I can be timid until I feel ignored, and then it's "Oh, *now* you wanna come with demands? Bye, girl."

Paul has asked me more than once why I have to be mad before I'll stand up for myself. The short answer is I don't know. My anxiety has made me need people for so long—my mom to answer her phone at work when I was having a panic attack as a teen; my sister to pick me up from high school so I didn't have to be home alone; my dad to leave work early and drive me to therapy; my husband to endure my temper when I seem angry but am actually overwhelmed. Maybe I'm scared I'll lose my life rafts if I offend the wrong people.

But there's more, underneath, tangled up, that I wish weren't true. I want people to like me, and to like Black people, even if they can't save me from panic or worse. I remember standing in my mostly Black Catholic church growing up, looking around when it was time to acknowledge first-time guests. They'd wave their hands and receive a ribbon or small gift from an usher. There I'd stand in the pew, often in Umbros and sneakers before tennis or soccer practice, under an embroidered Black Jesus tapestry hanging above our altar, hoping that if I smiled enough the white visitors would stay. I wanted them to know we liked them. We were good. Worthy.

How could I explain that to Paul? He'd gone to school with mostly white kids too, and while he knew how to code switch, he didn't seem to operate from such a deep need for acceptance.

"I think we're ready to go home," Paul told the lactation consultant. I was grateful he spoke for us.

We had a baby whose suck would probably strengthen over time, and we could feed him using the squeeze-and-spoon method until then. We'd figure it out. We'd done this baby thing before.

But we'd never had *this* baby before.


Before I even saw our firstborn's face, I heard the neonatologist at my feet ask, "Who has the hazel eyes?" Eliot was all gorgeous, always has been, a face of absolute symmetry and depth, with eyes of lightning that make you wonder what else God has up his sleeve.

Paged at the end of active labor, the neonatologist grabbed the baby and tried to suck meconium from her lungs but found none. The baby cried, a good sign. A nurse cleaned her, wrapped her, handed her to me, and I stared at her gelled eyelids and sweet lips until she began to blow little bubbles, until her lips started to look more purplish than rose. They took her to the nursery before rushing her to the neonatal intensive care unit. A doctor with pixied black hair walked in, pulled a curtain behind her, and sat down next to my bed.

"Your daughter was having a little trouble breathing." Her face looked so serious—too serious for a baby who was still alive. Maybe even too serious for a baby I didn't feel completely attached to yet.

That night, Paul wheeled me down to the NICU. We learned how to wash with individually wrapped yellow scrubbers and nail cleaners and found Eliot's room. The light was off, the space empty.

"We moved her to this room over here," said a nurse, rescuing us from our worst thoughts.

Inside, our baby lay with a clear globe over her head, antibiotics and fluids traveling through her veins, monitors speaking up for her body. It wasn't the Zoloft or anything I'd eaten. She had pneumonia, and no one could tell us why. They couldn't find the bacteria or source, but we would take her home in a week, and she would be healed. Once she passed her hearing screening as a toddler, none of this NICU stay would matter. It would be noted in her records, a story we'd share now and then with other parents, and a reminder to me of God's grace through medicine. But Eliot's sickness was a finite event, if a little mysterious in origin. Not something that haunted and confused or persisted. Eliot's illness was not something I worried I'd caused.

So we *thought* we'd done this before.

My pregnancy with Tophs, for the most part, mirrored my pregnancy with Eliot: three trimesters of round-the-clock nausea; unremarkable prenatal appointments and screenings; and, finally, slow, painful contractions that danced between the six- to eight-minute marks and left me, after a day of laboring at home, begging for an epidural. Thankfully, Paul learned his lesson the first time around, so when my uterus began to contract with Tophs, he did not suggest a trip to Home Depot to take my mind off the pain.

I respect but do not pretend to understand women who forgo the Great Epidural. *The baby will come out of a hole? One of mine?* When a nurse on the night shift watched me ball up in pain with a contraction while in labor with Tophs, she moved her hand along my side and commanded, "Let the pain wash over you like a wave." She was dead to me.

For me, labor is an ugly body contortion and lack of control—pelvic and mental—and the lack of belief that I can endure. Each time, my mind runs loops, gets stuck around the thought that this crashing of my uterus against the walls of my body will never end and I will have to ask someone to help me die. The thought is no less potent just because it's irrational. Finally, a doctor in scrubs pushes a cart in, cleans my back with iodine, and presses a needle into my spine. Somehow I don't contract as I'm hunched over. I don't make the needle zigzag across my back or paralyze me, and even though I fear the metallic taste in my mouth is the harbinger of an allergic reaction, relief soon sweeps over me, and I cease to care about much of anything. Nothing seems urgent or dangerous. I begin to text my friends.

When the labor and delivery nurse held a printout from the monitor in her hands and said, "We're keeping an eye on the baby's heart rate. He's had some decelerations," I didn't ask questions. It was as though the epidural had numbed my amygdala too. Paul might have asked the nurse to elaborate, but I stayed beneath the shield of complacency. They would let us know if the baby was in serious trouble. They would do their best to save him. This gift of mine, this circus trick, is what one therapist called *detachment*.

But I'm also able to drift mentally because I trust Paul. When I'm most fearful or in pain, he's the one I want next to me. I realized this when I gave birth to Eliot. Paul, with his slightly bowed legs and calm nature, with his prepacked snacks and typed birth plan, was the one I needed. As he leaned in to tell me I was beautiful and strong, I believed him. My parents could hold the baby and help around the house, but I no longer needed them in the same way. Paul and I had made something together.

When it came time to deliver Tophs, my short OB with a graying comb-over, who still rode his bike to work, walked into the room.

"You've got about fifteen minutes, because my shift is ending," the nurse joked.

I tried to push, without any real feeling, as the nurse and Paul each held one of my legs. They counted down, maybe twice, maybe three times, before Tophs slid out. I had pushed for over two hours with Eliot.

"He's a little blue but fine," my OB said.

They placed him on my chest, a blanket over his back. He was tiny. Bluer than Eliot. A little more wrinkled and dry. He had these ridges that crossed his abdomen and made him look oddly muscular. But he and his sister shared the same small bridgeless nose and perfectly proportioned lips.

I must have seen his eyes. But when I think of newborn Tophs, I only see them closed. He was supposed to "pink up" on my chest. The mother's chest can cure most ills, but after a few minutes, a nurse put him under the warmers. He was breathing just fine, but I wasn't able to turn him pink.

My mom asked about my health the minute I was born. I know because my parents saved an audiocassette recording of my birth. Side A holds my birth, which is really a tape of my mother—her pain, her body, her questions—until I show up at the very end.

"You all right?" the doctor asks my mother. "It's a baby girl!"

My high-pitched "Waaaaaaahs!" take over, the sound of light bulbs breaking beneath a cloth.

"Is she okay?" Mom asks.

"Oh, she's fine," he says.

"Was the baby in real good condition?" she asks again.

"Oh yeah. My goodness, yeah. Comin' out screamin' like that."

In the first and fifth minutes after birth, doctors check a newborn's vitals and determine an Apgar score. My own score, based on my heart rate, breathing, responsiveness, muscle tone, and skin coloration, was normal—a seven or eight. Anyone in the delivery room can tell you Apgar scores determine a baby's need for *urgent* or immediate medical attention. They don't tell you much about the baby's long-term health. My sisters and I all had normal Apgar scores even though we reacted differently to life outside the womb. Mom says Autumn, the firstborn, emerged excited, her tiny eyes peering all around. My middle sister, Sienna, came out quietly and slept. I arrived screaming.

The first night after Tophs's birth, I sent him to the nursery, knowing I was bucking up against an unwritten rule of this hospital that mothers, exhausted mothers, should want to keep their babies with them as much as possible. *Breast-is-best, skin-to-skin, the-nursery-is-only-for-sick-babies* hummed the walls of the maternity ward.

A young, blonde nurse burst into my room in the middle of the night, rolling a swaddled Tophs in a clear bassinet in front of her. She moved like a big sister flipping on the lights and slamming the door to wake you up. "He's been in the nursery for almost three hours. If you want to breastfeed him, you need to keep trying."

Right. Keep trying. I sat up, feeling drugged. I held him to one breast, then the other, as his lips closed around me, then slackened. I have no idea where I put the baby when I finished.

The next night, I think I kept Tophs in the room with me. I slept the kind of sleep that ends in sweating off some of your body weight, the extra fluids from forty weeks of growing a whole human. When my OB, his blue eyes kind and certain, appeared at my bedside to take Tophs away in the morning, I couldn't remember the last time a nurse had woken me up or checked on me. "We'll numb the area and give him some sugar water," he said, before taking him to be circumcised.

I should have spoken up then, should have asked for one minute, even if he didn't latch, to hold Tophs to my breast.

After they left, a nurse walked in, her movements brisk. "I heard in the nursery that you haven't fed him for several hours."

*She'd heard?* They were talking about me in the nursery. I tried to explain: I was asleep. He was asleep. I'm so tired.

*You're not doing this right,* is all I took from her tone and the apparent buzz around the incubators. I had failed him already. In my most vulnerable moments, I come back to this and wonder: What if all my son's maladies and challenges can be traced to this one mistake, this gap in feeding, that lay squarely on my chest? What if, in those early hours, I damaged a pathway, a circuit, that never quite repaired itself? What if I caused a deficit he never recovered from? In a matter of seconds, I become Alice, shrinking down to the ground with just a bite, and I have to remind myself there's no evidence to support that claim. It's best buried forever.

After our time with the lactation consultant, we were discharged with Tophs, tiny in his new black car seat, wearing a terry cloth Baby Gap outfit that dwarfed him—who knew I'd need preemie clothes? Whereas Eliot left the NICU looking giant, a healthy eight-pound baby who didn't belong, Tophs left the hospital having lost 9 percent of his body weight. He really was a five-pounder then, the son of a questionable mother, a boy who passed every newborn screening, who was a little blue but fine.

His first medical chart, labeled "Newborn Progress Notes," tells the abbreviated story of Boy Harris's first forty-eight hours of life. It lists metrics such as his length, head and chest circumferences, bilirubin levels, vaccinations, and Apgar scores. Eliot's scores were a six and then eight, as she appeared to breathe better at the five-minute mark before she, once again, struggled. Tophs scored an eight and nine. Rarely does a baby score a perfect ten. In other words, Tophs nailed his first tests.

Those early postpartum days are such a blur, the hospital a

strange and sterile place to transition into a new stage of mother-hood, and it's nearly impossible to know what each heel prick or injection means. These brief records have kept me from believing stories that are convenient but just not true—stories that could have solved the medical mysteries that would unfold in my son's life, the kind that would have made everyone's job easier.

When I wonder if he was crying all night and I just slept through it, I'm comforted by a nurse practitioner's handwritten note: *breastfeeding off to slow start: sleepy!*

See? I say to someone, no one, myself: he was sleepy!

Her note continues: *small—well-developed male; mild jaundice.*

"He was a little blue but perfectly healthy," I wrote on the first page of a Moleskine journal.

Tophs, a small, sleepy baby who should get some sunlight. You and I have proof. If any problems existed in the beginning, they must have been well hidden, wedged deep beneath the cover of my son's beautiful body.

4

There's one clue something was wrong that I can't possibly remember. But it's been told and retold to me, wallpapered to
my mind:

Five weeks after I was born, my mom started working nights
at the post office. She'd applied the year before and had finally
moved off the waitlist. She and Dad now had three children and a
mortgage on a small ranch where relatives rotated in and out of the
basement, according to need.

Back then, a man could make a decent living working an indus-
trial job. The Westside of Columbus was home to a huge General
Motors plant that resembled a prison complex from the outside
with its high fences and bland brick. It was the kind of place where
guys wore blue jeans, carried pairs of orange earplugs and goggles
at all times, and packed their lunches in coolers. Dad worked second shift and overtime whenever he could, assembling door locks

and grinding excess metal off welded doorframes, standing at sta-
tions, some manned by robots, others by people. He punched in
around three o'clock each afternoon, played cards with the fellas
on his evening break, and clocked out long after sunset.

Both my parents, who met in middle school, excelled in aca-
demics and attended college but didn't finish. Mom had worked
office jobs but took the greatest pride in teaching her daughters to
read before kindergarten. When the post office called to offer her
a position, she fought with herself and then Dad and then herself
again; they needed the money, but, in her gut, she didn't feel ready
to leave me.

Within two weeks of Mom working nights, I stopped taking
a bottle. She tried all the nurses' suggestions: flat 7-Up, popsicles,
Pedialyte. By the time she reached the on-call doctor, I wouldn't
stop screaming.

"Is that the baby in the background?" he asked.

"Yes, that's what I've been telling you," Mom said. "Something's not right with her." I see her holding the phone between
her shoulder and ear, the cord keeping her close to the kitchen wall,
as she shushes and bounces me.

"My goodness. If that's her, you need to take her to the ER."

After two days of IVs to rehydrate me, after Mom basically told
her boss he could go to hell for asking her to leave me there alone,
Children's Hospital released me to the care of Dr. Dawdy, my first
and only pediatrician. He looked like Phil Donahue and wore a toy
monkey clipped to his stethoscope. Sitting on a black stool with
one leg propped up on the other knee, he listened and never rushed
away after writing a prescription.

"What we're looking at here," he told my mom, "is separation anxiety." He explained that I hadn't experienced enough bonding time with my mom and that separation had affected me more than the next baby.

My mother took the blame, courted undeserved guilt, for making a tough decision that wasn't wrong. And as I grew older, I was most often her quiet but pleasant baby girl, the one who sang "Teeto Teeto Little Tar" and recited my ABCs for praise on side B of that audiocassette tape. My favorite photograph shows me at three wearing frizzy, braided pigtails, a necklace of dyed macaroni, and green Mickey Mouse sunglasses. I'm brandishing a Barbie and smiling, my bare brown legs showing beneath a faded birthday T-shirt. It would be about thirteen years before I'd get my official diagnosis, and who can say if my anxiety was always present, even at birth, waiting for my mother's job offer, or a conversation on death, or dimming store lights, to reveal itself?

"I thought it was temporary," Mom has said.

Tophs's slow weight gain as an infant didn't slap us in the face. Somewhere between six and twelve months, his growth curve began to flatten, even though his cheeks still looked stuffed with marshmallows. He started crawling at twelve months, on the day of his birthday party when his library storytime friends arrived, so it was hard to tell if he was simply burning more calories than before.

We saw Dr. Quillian about once a month for weight checks as Tophs began to track under the fifth percentile for height and weight. I'd show up to those appointments with Eliot and Tophs and our monster truck stroller. The nurse would sit Tophs on the scale as he looked up at a pinwheel she spun. After, she'd offer to push the stroller as I wrapped Tophs in a muslin blanket and followed her through the hallways decorated with hundreds of baby pictures and Christmas cards.

I'm not sure who was more pleased, Tophs or me, to see Dr. Quillian push through the door and sit at her computer.

"Hello, Harris family!" she'd say. Eliot just stared, but Tophs would grin and bounce. Everything about Dr. Quillian, from her simple black slacks to her marled gray sweaters to her shiny black clogs, gave off a casually cool vibe I admired.

As she felt Tophs's stomach or moved his legs up and down, his mouth would break wide open, exposing more gums than teeth. "You love Dr. Quillian," I'd say. Eliot, like me, had always been guarded around others; I marveled at this child who freely expressed interest in people.

"I mean, he's just not sickly," Dr. Quillian would say. This is the line I remember most from those weight checks, because it was true.

At thirteen months, Tophs sat like a brown cherub on our living room rug in a Certified Hunk raglan tee. Everything about him was round and brown, all soft corners and baby curls. He seemed to live his life, planted on our floor, not yet walking, fully aware of the toys and sounds around him. Eliot plopped down next to him and waved her hands. "Boo!" she said, and his whole body erupted in giggles. He reached for her, his first way of saying, "Again!" No one was more fun than his big sister, and no one freed her up to be herself quite like Tophs.

As Dr. Quillian urged me to make butter Tophs's best friend, I texted my family on a thread: "At least one of us can drink all the milkshakes we want!"

"Let's see you back in a month" was never an alarming state-ment. Someone I trusted kept track of Tophs. He was safe.

At home, I figured out how to peel and cut an avocado, placing soft cubes on his tray. He picked up pieces between his short, thick fingers, palming them into his mouth. He chewed, made a face, flaring his nostrils, but swallowed. Hey, even I didn't like avocado. He drank almond and whole milk, ate plain bagels with melted butter. The kid preferred goldfish crackers over everything, but he wasn't *that* picky. We could do this.

At sixteen months, Tophs's medical records list "poor weight gain in child" for the first time. His height and weight put him un-der the first percentile, while his head was in the seventy-seventh. But he babbled and said "Mama." He initiated games of hide-and-seek. He used a tiny metal spatula to stir and eat pretend food at his wooden play stove. Dr. Quillian's note reads: *Given his normal exam and general state of great health, I feel this is most likely an issue of inadequate calories rather than a pathological process.*

Said another way: we can fix this.


When I was ten or eleven, Mom told a story from the passenger's seat of our van about choking on a piece of apple skin as a girl. That story led to another, as she and Dad tried to remember how my great-uncle Bernard, from whom Dad got his middle name, had choked on a hot dog or bottle cap and died. I pictured a round man with creamy brown skin and gray hair, his belly large, leaning back in a dining chair, panicked, air trapped above and beneath a bottle cap perfectly rounded to the sputtering man's throat.

I started walking home from elementary school for lunch every day and warming a can of Campbell's tomato soup on the stove so I wouldn't have to eat anything that could get trapped in my throat. Sometimes Dad slept close by in my parents' bedroom after his late shift, but other times I ate alone, and I couldn't risk choking with no one there to call for help.

I must have cloaked the fear, even with my mother. Why didn't I tell her about the apple slice and then Uncle Bernard and then me? Instead, I told my parents I could feel something stuck in my throat, almost like a hair, which wasn't a lie but wasn't the whole truth. "Maybe we should take her to the emergency room," my dad said one night when we picked him up from the factory. My mind fixated on his suggestion, and I wondered if we should head there straight away.

We didn't drive to the ER that night, but Mom did take me to Dr. Dawdy, who ordered a barium swallow test. I can taste the chalky white drink, feel the fear of climbing onto a large exam table, but also the comfort in knowing people in white coats were inspecting my insides. "There is no evidence of stricture, obstruction, or hernia," the record reads. The impression was normal.

The same week, I saw a cardiologist. Sometimes the noticing centered on my chest. My heart pounded, beat too fast. The bone that ran between my barely formed breasts ached. The doctor asked about the type of pain I felt. Did I feel it when I played tennis? Not really. Did changing positions help? Sometimes. A nurse placed cold heart-shaped stickers around my chest and connected an array of thin wires to me. The readout was perfect. Relief broke over me with each good-news call from Dr. Dawdy or his nurse, until the next thought took hold.

When the sister of a family friend died of a brain aneurysm, pain piercing her skull as she showered, I superimposed my tension headaches over her tragedy: I would soon die, without warning. I would die, and they would place my body in one of those black bags I saw being rolled out of a long white car when we picked up Mom from the back of the city hospital, where she worked as a medical transcriptionist. I hated picking her up back there. Death felt contagious; if I saw too much, if I got too close, I would be next.

"If you hold someone's hand when they die, will you die too?" Tophs asked me last year.

By nineteen months, Tophs would clap and stomp around the middle of the exam room, singing nonsense songs for Dr. Quillian when she greeted him. She wrote: *We will continue to monitor this and if at any point parents or I feel worried that he is "failing to thrive" in any way we will obtain labs. Given that his [physical exam] and development and energy is so normal, I think the likelihood of finding anything wrong in the lab or workup is low.*

He was normal, we were normal. We were doing normal really well. A few times a week, we'd walk to the dining hall, where Paul would make the kids waffles while I grabbed a booth. Busy undergrad students stopped and looked up from their phones to smile and wave. Every now and then, they'd offer to babysit. We'd let the kids finish with soft-serve ice cream in cake cones, just as Paul and I had finished off most meals in college. These were the sweet rituals, the norms that never quite disappeared but would become loaded with new meaning as we searched for the cause of Tophs's symptoms. Ice cream is no longer just ice cream when it's the last thing your son ate before he woke up, a shell of himself. The aftertaste lingers, sweet some days, more bitter on others, your taste shaped by just how hopeful or uncertain you are in the moment. Whether you think you're leaving the Unsettling Place for good or whether you've soberly begun to understand that being unsettled is the same as being home.

Marriage and growing a family aren't simple endeavors for anyone, but Paul has always carried himself with a light and easy confidence I'd noticed back when we were students. We played tennis one night under the lights, and he stopped for a moment, pretending to sniff his armpits. "Don't worry, baby," he said, looking straight at me. "My sweat smells like potpourri." Of course he was joking, but his eyes almost made me believe him. Paul's optimism, and my belief over time that he could handle almost anything, lifted and stabilized me before Tophs ever got sick. After I'd adjusted to being a mom of toddlers rather than a teenaged hottie walking across campus, I'd come to enjoy being back at UVA— this overlaying of our past with our present seemed like a gift, a chance to create new life against an already meaningful backdrop. It was during this time, still in the Before, when I didn't yet understand I could interrupt Paul's steady and joyful nature without fearing I might somehow lose him.

One of these very *normal* days, before the first medical crisis, before I encountered questions that served as both guideposts and trapdoors or knew life could feel like one large waiting room, I pulled into our parking spot at the bottom of the hill and unlatched my sleeping boy from his car seat. Tophs was big enough to feel heavy but small enough to cradle in my arms. It was the kind of day that earns Charlottesville a place on lists of the most beautiful cities. The sun comes to you clean and dry, filtered through leaves, and the air stands still without stifling you, having shed its humidity. I walked with him in my arms, past the first garden and the basketball hoop, and stopped on the stairs.

I stopped, and held my boy, and this sense overwhelmed me—it seeped into my skin, traveled the length of my limbs before settling down into my rib cage, finding its center near my lungs, making a nest in my chest cavity.

But it did not hurt. It sang—a gentle, binding lyric made of sunflower stalks and bone: *Enjoy him. Hold him. Stay right here.*

Only the two of us were there, and maybe God. Was this the Holy Spirit, settling like a dove? As I moved up the stairs, I couldn't deny the peace falling in thin quilts over me. This wasn't scary, whatever it was. Wasn't meant to instill fear or evoke panic. I could not even *will* my body to fear. Whatever this was, this premonition, this message, this prayer—I was meant to love this boy and hold tight to his joy.

I told no one, not even Paul. I acted as though giving words to the memory might change its very form. As though sharing might expose the worst of me, the sin of hyperbole, and leave me alone, set apart from everything good we'd made.

# 5

Tophs was just two months out from his two-year-old checkup with Dr. Quillian the morning of April 1. The morning when he awoke but didn't stir, in the haunting way that turns a real child into a doll. The morning Paul handed him to me and I pulled him close, without knowing anything but a few simple truths.

After that trip to the ER, I didn't feel our world was crumbling; it wasn't that dramatic. But as I bathed Tophs at home the night after he was discharged, I noticed one side of his scrotum looked swollen. I thought of all the pulling and taping the nurses and I had done to secure that plastic bag. Had we caused this? I showed Dr. Quillian the next day. "It looks like he has a small inguinal hernia." Not an emergency, but he'd need surgery. Our boy wasn't falling apart. Plenty of baby boys develop these hernias, considered a quick fix. But I couldn't ignore how the last few days felt like a terrible prank, with his blood sugar tanking on April Fool's Day, and his body bulging, ever so slightly, under running water the next.

Days later, I stood in the apartment hallway, staring at a pink silver-dollar mark on the rough gray wall. One of the kids must have smashed Play-Doh against the textured cinder block. I had tried to scrape it off but couldn't do anything about the bits that had hardened within the grit of the wall.

"How's he doing?" Dr. Quillian's voice, light and airy, flitted into my ear from the phone.

"He seems okay," I told her. "You know Tophs, he's back to dancing around, and we're giving him a snack before bed."

And then the same doctor, the same light overtones of her voice giving way to a slower, more reserved undertone, a shark beneath the boat, an audible transition I hadn't yet learned to identify. "We got the results of those labs sent out to Mayo, and it looks like Christopher's carnitine levels were low."

I knew she was smart. Hadn't she studied at Stanford? She must have meant "creatinine" or "creatine." But she didn't correct her mistake. She briefly explained that carnitine affects how the body processes fat and energy. "The note here from Genetics says, 'Provide clinical information to aid in interpretation.' So I've sent a note over to the chief. He's a brilliant guy, been around forever. I'll find out what he thinks we should do next."

What *he* thinks . . . Immediately a white-haired man with glasses and bulky, black-soled shoes shot to the top of my *People Who Know* list. He would make sense of this. If we could just touch the hem of his lab coat.

"In the meantime, don't Google it. This could be something that resolves on its own. It could be a fluke."

As the call ended, I moved farther away from the place of the mundane, where pink crap gets stuck to the wall, where the doctor calls to say everything will be okay. In the After, even an experienced pediatrician like Dr. Quillian can't promise she knows just what to do or has ever seen this before.

*But what if something really is wrong?* If questions were birthstones, this would be mine. I remember standing against a wall of blue lockers on the first floor of my high school, imagining a boy falling to the ground, EMTs interrupting his boy scout meeting with CPR, pulling him back from the other side after his heart had stopped beating. He was alive, we were told, would one day return to school, but I stayed in the *how* of it all. As in, how could a young, healthy boy almost perish without reason?

I tried not to look at the room where I believed the troop meeting occurred. I didn't want to catch the Near Death. When my own heart seemed to beat double or skip and drop to my gut, I told my mom, who called Dr. Dawdy, who referred me to a different cardiologist, a man with glasses whose words gently sliced the air.

"I am not worried about Taylor" is the kind of thing I remember him saying, the kind of thing most doctors have said most of my life.

I don't have all my medical records, but I'm certain of this: After an echocardiogram, the doctor diagnosed me with a mitral valve prolapse. The flaps over one of my valves didn't always close completely, and sometimes a little blood leaked back through, called regurgitation. *How disgusting*, I thought.

As a teenager, I didn't think to ask him if the prolapsed valve might have been there before, if the previous doctor might have missed it. Had I been right all along? Could fear, even fear tinged with the irrational, help me discover deeper truths about my body? Or had my anxiety somehow created this minor flaw, my thoughts summoning my body to transform?

More than affirmation or curiosity, I felt a release initially. I could still play tennis every day; I would just take antibiotics before the dentist cleaned my teeth. My mom had a mitral valve prolapse too. It ran in the family.

Yet I am also certain of this: after the safe diagnosis, after my lungs expanded with relief, I started worrying again. I noticed every way my heart galloped or dropped. A note from the cardiologist to Dr. Dawdy after a follow-up visit reads: *[S]he simply has an increased awareness of myocardial function. No arrhythmias were noted.* Around this time, Dr. Dawdy's nurse returned a call from my mom about the latest litany of symptoms. He didn't want to bring us in or refer me out. Instead, his nurse relayed a message: "Taylor is noticing too much about her body." Said another way: *There's nothing wrong.* What I heard: *Don't be foolish. Calm down. You're overreacting.*

Looking back, I see myself feeling out the boundaries of fear, marking the places where shame crept in. I had noticed things about my body that didn't matter. But noticing had also led me to truth, to blood leaking backward in my heart.

*Even as I lose sleep, even as I panic,*
*have I, sometimes, found*
*a thing worth finding?*

Before I ever picked up a Bible as a college student, my body penned a psalm. For me as a young adult, for me as a mother.

I tried to take Dr. Quillian's advice and be the parent who didn't rush to lay test results at the altar of Google. But not long after the call, I slipped behind the desktop Mac in our living room, typing singular conditions into the search box: *ketotic hypoglycemia; inguinal hernia.* Then *carnitine deficiency.*

"Carnitine is a natural substance acquired mostly through diet," the National Institutes of Health site read. I kept searching for connections. "Signs and symptoms of primary carnitine deficiency typically appear during infancy or early childhood and can include severe brain dysfunction (encephalopathy), a weakened and enlarged heart (cardiomyopathy), confusion, vomiting, muscle weakness, and low blood sugar (hypoglycemia) "

This *was* early childhood. He'd vomited a few days before his blood sugar dropped. His carnitine was low. What about the way his heart had pounded in his chest that morning?

"All individuals with this disorder are at risk for heart failure, liver problems, coma, and sudden death." I leaned in closer. There it was. I'd found it. All individuals—sudden death. I could lose him. Maybe that's what the moment on the stairs, months before, had meant. Drink him in, all of him, while you can.

# 6

I drove to an old pharmacy I'd barely noticed before, a brick build-ing with white trim next to a Mexican restaurant. Dr. Quillian had called back with instructions from the geneticist: Tophs should start taking liquid carnitine. "Let me call around and find some-one that carries it," she'd said. "And just to warn you, it might make him smell like fish."

Inside, Tophs and Eliot grabbed at Melissa & Doug puzzles and stuffed beanie toys. I tried to corral them, to keep us quiet in this old-school setting where I didn't see any people of color. As lovely and quaint as Charlottesville can be, you can't forget that many businesses were *forced* to start serving Black people. The owners don't hang up signs anymore; you have to read faces.

Eliot usually listened to me, but Tophs had already started to keep me guessing. He didn't always respond to his name. As a newborn, he'd earned the nickname "Zen baby" from his first babysitter but was beginning to show an unpredictable edge. Eliot would listen, obey, eventually disobey, and then have a complete meltdown. Tophs, on the other hand, would half listen, dance, pull things off the shelf, tantrum, and attempt a headstand.

Only a few creams and soaps fell off the bottom shelf before we made it to the register. An employee prepared a bag for us behind the high counter. I peered over the top and into the shelves of bottles and boxes that lined the back walls.

*Excuse me, can I ask you something? Is this weird—us needing this drug? Does anyone else take it?* I wanted to ask. Instead I paid, took the medicine, and left.

*How serious is this?* The question I wanted, more and more, to ask strangers. I wanted measuring sticks, mile markers. "Always give your readers a signpost," my favorite writing instructor taught us in grad school. "They'll stick with you, but you have to let them know where you are." Where were my signposts?

Who was this baby boy Paul and I had made? A question that would rise time and time again to the top of my mind, gathering air like a balloon stretched thin.

He was, for a couple of weeks, a boy who smelled like fish. After several doses of the liquid carnitine, I leaned forward into the top of my son's smooth curls as he stood on a stone ledge next the sidewalk. Instead of coconut conditioner or a hint of salty sweat, I got the smell of iridescent fish laid out on ice in the local grocery store. My child didn't smell like my child but rather the thing that might fix him. If something were really wrong inside, if his metabolism couldn't do what God had designed metabolisms to do, would it be this obvious? Would finding a glitch be like seeing a boy but smelling a fish?

Tophs, of course, didn't care. He snuggled with his big sister in the hammock, poking at her belly as the two of them lay close as lovers, grinning. He had started to reach for Eliot, and nothing pleased me more. Paul—the guy who'd packed us a picnic basket with roses and sparkling cider for a date before I even agreed to be his girlfriend—and I had made them. Tophs loved to walk along the garden and jump off anything—a marble ledge, a concrete stair. Or he'd stand in the middle of the quad, vocalizing sounds to the beat of his body. It reminded us of the step shows of Black Greek letter organizations. "He's a step master just like his daddy," I joked with Paul, who had choreographed steps for his frat brothers back in the day.

By the time Paul and I started dating, he was a well-known Alpha at UVA but used his rhythm to draw me in rather than to excite a crowd. He pulled his green Honda Accord into my apartment complex one night, opened the car doors, and invited me to dance in the headlights to Musiq Soulchild. The boy was charming, not slippery but smooth. The first time I ever felt that shimmering jolt from Paul's body to mine, the night he touched my knee under a table, we were listening to artists at a local café. I kept the ticket stub in my box of special things, a reminder of our chemistry.

Secretly, I felt proud that I'd helped create a boy who had more rhythm than I did. A miniature Paul. What else might Tophs do better than me? With the help of Paul's genes, what talents might come naturally for him? And which of my genetic pitfalls might he avoid?


I was fourteen for the first significant event, the kind you share with every therapist as proof. During intake, you open your hand

and hold it forth, a memory stone laid in the riverbed of your past, a sort of memorial to, or witness of, fear.

My parents allowed each of us girls to take one big trip during high school. We couldn't really afford it, but they never wanted a lack of money or opportunity to limit us. With a good education, their strong-willed daughters could avoid the stumbling blocks that had tripped them up and contributed to their divorce when I was thirteen.

As the youngest by five years, I'd waited a long time for my turn, and I chose a spring break trip to Spain organized by my high school. My best friend, Lindsay, and I would spend a week walking the streets of Madrid and Toledo, visiting landmarks, staying in fancy hotels. When it was time, I stood under the flags of various nations hanging from the Columbus airport ceiling, my suitcase stuffed with clothes and a red pack of chewy Chips Ahoy cookies. The people buzzing about, moving with purpose, made me feel important.

Lindsay and I sat next to each other on the second, longer flight from New York, in the middle row of three, kids giddy with faux independence. A digital map above displayed the route we'd take across the Atlantic. The plane took off into the night, and I don't know where we were on the map—far over the water and deep into the black sky—when I felt my throat closing. My breaths shortened, black specks dotted my vision. I was dying. I needed an EpiPen, a doctor. We needed to land the plane. Needed out of here.

I woke Lindsay up, the space already spinning, the air dissolving around me. *I can't sleep. I need help. I don't feel well.* I'm not sure what I said to describe being swallowed by dread. *Gattaca* played again and again on the screens in front of us, and she must have lifted her head up and asked, "Are you okay? Do you wanna lay down?" As I lowered my head onto her lap, the world turned sideways, my lungs opened back up, my pulse relaxed into itself. I began to breathe and fell asleep.

Throughout the following week, as we ate at a buffet with paella or stood under the ceiling of a great cathedral or drove through a green countryside spotting sheep, thoughts multiplied in my body, spilling over: I was too far away from a hospital; an allergic reaction would kill me; I'd never return home alive.

I borrowed Lindsay's sunglasses as we toured, the temporary dimness dulling the panic, but when she wanted them back, I grew angry. And when she wanted to hang out with other classmates on the trip instead of staying safely in our hotel room, next to the phone, I felt betrayed. Overseas, Lindsay was my only security.

When I finally returned to Ohio, after days of my mom trying to have a prescription for a drug like Valium filled in Spain, I pushed Lindsay away. I wanted no part of abandonment or worry.

I felt silly worrying about how Tophs smelled when we were out, but I did. We constantly interacted with students and other faculty members, even on trips to the mailroom or the communal laundromat. What should I say to them? *We bathe him. I don't even eat fish. It's this medicine he takes, to fix a problem we're not sure he has. It may be a fluke. He might drop dead.* This inability to explain, whether to a make-believe inquisitor or a real friend, or even a physician trying to solve our case, has never truly disappeared. It shows up in special education meetings at his school, as we scramble to codify something that has been observed in reality but not yet named.

The hard-to-find liquid that pushed fish through the pores of my boy worked. Even after we stopped giving it to him and the smell faded, his carnitine levels stayed within a normal range. It hadn't necessarily been a fluke—he had two rounds of abnormal test results—but it wasn't necessarily a chronic problem either. Maybe his body just needed a hand to right itself. In the span of two months, we'd seen alarming hypoglycemia, a hernia, and a carnitine deficiency. What would come next?

While we waited for Tophs's body to give us more clues as to who he would be, we met my family in the Outer Banks for a week in May, near Tophs's second birthday. Mom always booked the house and drove down from Ohio with my stepdad, Bryan, whom she'd married during my first year of college. She also invited Dad. It sounds weird, but it sort of worked. We spent Thanksgivings together at one long table, and now that the three of us girls were grown and starting families of our own, we didn't have enough money or time to take separate vacations. So we all shared Moby Duck, a house on stilts within walking distance of the beach, and met up for dinners and trips to our favorite coffee shop.

Paul and I set out for the beach one afternoon with the kids and a cheap neon tent. I carried Tophs down the road, a navy sun hat shading his face. We passed the glamorous updated houses, then walked along the wooden ramp and down the stairs to the shore. Within five minutes of crossing the hot sand and setting up our tent, Tophs's cheeks burned red, his eyes barely moved, and his body felt heavy in my arms. I put him down on a towel in the corner of the tent for a moment; it wasn't far from his nap time. But when he stayed the same, unmoving, not sleeping, I picked him up and carried him back to the house, leaving Paul to watch Eliot play in the sand. Mom and Sienna felt his forehead and suggested an ice pack or a dose of Advil, and, after some fussing, he eventually fell asleep.

"It's like he wilted," I told Dr. Quillian when we got back to Charlottesville. We'd ended up taking Tophs to urgent care on vacation and learned he had an ear infection, but, again, we were left to sort out which symptoms might connect to which conditions. With Tophs, I wasn't ready to chalk everything up to an inflamed middle ear. There was the way he shivered after barely getting wet in the outdoor fountain of a shopping center. Or how he would lie down on the floor at home sometimes, not laughing or crying or sleeping. He looked more like a teenage boy who had flopped down on the couch and zoned out in front of the TV. Could it all be "True, True, and Unrelated?" as Dr. Quillian sometimes asked. The list continued to grow: hernia, hypoglycemia, carnitine deficiency, ear infection, possible heat intolerance, slow weight gain. Oh, and one more—an elevated level of AST, or aspartate aminotransferase, an enzyme that could be related to liver or muscle function. That was another abnormal result from Tophs's hospital stay, and no one could tell us if it mattered.

Not to mention the random, one-time occurrences. When Tophs was still a newborn, we used Paul's need for running shoes as an excuse to leave the house. The family-owned store is a Charlottesville favorite, and as the owner chatted with me and Paul scanned the shelves, Tophs's foot turned blue under my arm. The owner called his wife over. "Look at this," he said. "What do you think would cause this?" Within minutes, Tophs's foot had changed back to its healthy, reddish-brown tone, and we all shrugged it off. Taken one at a time, each symptom could seem trivial, certainly not life threatening. Taken as a whole, it felt like playing Twister on a Jackson Pollock painting.

The tone of Dr. Quillian's notes changed after Tophs's second birthday. After we returned from the beach, she wrote: *I am still concerned that something may be somewhat amiss in terms of a metabolic or endocrine etiology of his symptoms. His only persistent lab abnormality is a very mildly elevated AST, which may or may not be clinically significant.*

*May or may not be clinically significant.* Within those words I imagined a strict dichotomy. Over time, with the help of doctors, we would sort the symptoms appropriately. We would find what mattered.

*While most of patient's workup has been reassuring,* Dr. Quillian's note read, *there are still questions.*

We lived five minutes from a large university hospital staffed with specialists who, I imagined, spent their careers answering tough questions. The chief pediatric geneticist was one of them.

"Tell me what's been going on," he asked.

"As you know, he had the hypoglycemic episode on April 1." In so many conversations, Paul took the lead and I filled in details. I was more than happy to save my words. But as a stay-at-home mom with a tendency to *notice*, I did most of the talking during Tophs's medical appointments. I needed Paul's stable presence more than his voice. I also needed him to keep the kids from licking the floor or opening the big red box filled with used needles.

We placed Tophs on the exam table, and I waited—not exactly for a ticker-tape parade or the four horsemen to ride—but for the big *ah-ha*. Instead, the doctor crossed his arms, leaned against the table, and turned to us. "It's encouraging that his levels went up on the liquid carnitine. I don't think he's got a severe uptake deficiency."

My shoulders relaxed a bit as he pulled us up from the dangerous waters of sudden-death risk. *So what* does *he have?* I didn't ask.

"Let's repeat the labs today just to make sure his levels are still fine, and if they are, I think we keep moving forward as normal."

As normal. "So he can have surgery for his hernia?" I *did* ask that. The surgeon wanted more information before putting Tophs under anesthesia.

"If these levels check out, I think he's fine to have surgery." The appointment lasted about twenty minutes, and there was no *ah-ha*, but the chief of Genetics had ruled out the worst.

Paul and I left the hospital. We hadn't yet learned to smother our expectations before "big" appointments or turn to each other with our pain as parents. Hadn't learned that disappointment could be sacred. So we walked, mostly in silence, exchanging comments about dinner and work meetings, warning the kids to stay on the sidewalk.

Part of me knew I should be grateful. The other parts swelled with hunger. We had entered the uncertain waters of "weird but not necessarily dangerous" in which doctors guide the skiff and check their notes, gathering samples along the shore to file in a box we'd assumed would be marked *Answers* but instead is labeled *Interesting*. We could not be mad—how could we be mad?—because they were trying their best, and our son was safe enough, and what had we been promised, anyhow?


When I became a mother, I did not outline a Theology on Children, Medicine, and Health; nonetheless, there it was, sprouting limbs alongside the baby. It had grown up with me, from the time

Dr. Dawdy prescribed pink amoxicillin to cure my strep throat. It expanded and shifted over time to include Rachel, my first consistent therapist, who calmed my panic attacks with an SSRI and cognitive behavioral therapy; it made room for Jesus, to whom I cried while in the throes of anxiety and depression as a college student. It grew again when I carried my eight-pound firstborn home from the NICU without any lasting effects from pneumonia. It took a blow and reimagined itself when, after having prayed that my baby would not develop anxiety like mine, Eliot spent a year of preschool standing in the corner, too scared to move or speak.

In this theology, illness wasn't necessarily our fault, and miraculous healing didn't always occur. But God provided doctors and medicine, and for most of the health challenges we faced, if you called the right people and asked the right questions, made the right appointments and stayed the course, you would reach a satisfying end. If you turned over enough stones, you would find an answer.

Or, as Dr. Quillian said during one of our conversations, "We'll figure this out. Sometimes it takes a while to crack the code. I've had patients where it's taken even a year or more. But we'll figure it out."

Some days I would do anything to go back, to have the ability to rest in the hammock of those words again. It'd be a fool's errand, I know.

7

We did get a label sometimes—a true black-and-white name proven by numbers and codified standards, like "failure to thrive." Before Tophs's hernia surgery, we visited an endocrinologist with straight, black hair and crystal eyes who used the term. "Look how his growth velocity has slowed," she said, pointing to the graph on her computer. Apparently, two is a really big deal in pediatrics. Like if a kid hasn't gotten his stuff together after twenty-four months on the outside, doctors start to worry.

That day, she taught me how to use a glucometer to measure Tophs's blood sugar at home. This was a way to track his glucose when he didn't quite seem like himself, to search for a correlation. I'd do it, I told her, would prick his finger when something felt "off" and let the drop of pooled blood slide its way up the monitoring stick. I didn't tell her I was less and less certain when things were "off" and when they were just Tophs.

Yet even if his growth was abnormal now, there was still a chance Tophs would catch up one day. The endocrinologist called it constitutional growth delay. He might not play center in the NBA, but five-foot-eight was nothing to complain about. The failure-to-thrive diagnosis, given to a kid who bopped his head to Mike Posner's "Cooler Than Me" and taught me how to take a screenshot on my iPhone, could mean next to nothing in a few years. It could almost vanish.

In a video of Tophs, taken the day after his successful hernia surgery in July, he's squatting barefoot on our living room rug in white-and-green striped shorts and a navy polo shirt. From the side, it's easy to see how much shorter his feet are than the distance from his forehead to the back of his head. But he looks perfect with the sun streaming in behind him, a bronzed Lilliputian lifeguard on summer break.

When the video starts, he pops up to standing, and as Mike Posner sings the opening line of "Cooler Than Me," Tophs's eyes widen with recognition and his mouth drops open before his lips pucker into a fish face. For a moment, he's caught between watching the computer monitor and wanting to say something. He chooses the monitor. He waits four beats, cocks both elbows back, looks to the side, and begins a slight bounce, his feet never leaving the ground, as though he's warming up. And then it really begins—he's feeling it, and he raises his left arm and swings it across his body to the right side, does the same with his right arm before bringing his arms straight up in the air, alternating them to the beat. He throws in a little swag—steps side to side, holds his right arm in the air for two beats, his wrist bent, like a basketball player showing off after a sweet three-pointer. Then he starts it all over. It's a dance of his own creation, a mix between the Carlton and yet-to-come Milly Rock, and he's in complete control, even if he's choreographing on the fly.

Tophs improvises without need for words or explanation. It's so natural; he doesn't fight for attention or try to outdo Eliot, who is a good dancer in her own right. When Tophs dances, I know him. I don't have any questions except "What song do you want to hear next?" This is the Tophs I brought to appointments on just about every floor of the children's hospital. This is the Tophs who charmed every nurse and doctor he met. Yet it was here, within this body of great symmetry, balance, and beauty, we kept finding evidence that something was amiss.

In another video, taken a few months later, Tophs is standing before me in the kitchen, shaking, a drop of milk visible under his neck. He's woken up from his afternoon nap and wears a long-sleeved cotton shirt and pants. He's holding one of those take-and-toss plastic cups with a lid and straw, filled with milk. His eyes look wet, but he's not crying, and his nose runs. Toddlers' noses are faucets, but the unsettling part is the way that cup shakes in his hands as his lips vibrate, and his eyes search me.

"You okay, Tophs?" I ask.

"Uh," he shakes his head no, makes the beginning sound of a cry, then stops and looks down.

"Are you cold?"

He looks at me, opens his mouth slightly, then looks away, teeth chattering.


"What's wrong, sweetheart?" Mom was always the one who talked me down.

I'd left my math class, snuck down to the payphone in my high school lobby, and called her at work. One minute, I'd been staring at the chalkboard, the next I couldn't breathe. Small chalk clouds had found their way into my body, coated my lungs, making the sacs too sticky for air.

"I'm right here. Just breathe, honey." With Mom's guidance, the walls of the school, like the walls of my chest, would open back up, and I could continue to keep my secret. As a class president, standout tennis player, and straight-A student, I would have died if my peers knew I was crazy.

But when the panic attacks started to come several times a day; when I refused to stay home by myself for even fifteen minutes while Mom ran to the post office; when I started missing school but obsessively collecting my homework assignments, Dr. Dawdy referred me to Rachel.

Dad left his shift at the factory early to pick me up from school in time to get downtown to Children's Hospital by four o'clock. Sometimes he played contemporary Christian music or Focus on the Family when, previously, we'd listened to R&B in the car. He seemed way more into Jesus since the divorce. "Thank you, Lord, for this beautiful day," he'd say aloud, looking out the window, and I thought he'd lost it. But he showed up every week, as though making up for what he'd missed by working so much when I was younger. As a young father, did Dad think financial security, just getting one or two paychecks ahead, could give him the sort of relief that a normal CT scan or EKG gave me? Maybe if his checking account looked better, his marriage, his parenting, his life would all fall into place.

As a sixteen-year-old, I wanted him near but not in the room.

I left him in the lobby with his thick, leather-bound study Bible. I was old enough to tell my story. I would tell her about Spain. And, of course, the trip to New York just weeks before, how I'd won tickets to the ESPY Awards for an essay I'd written, how everything on that flight back home broke and stayed broken:

We'd flown first class because Dad worked part-time at the airport, but what should have been a treat felt more like a dare. The first row of the America West jet was too close to the cockpit. As with hospitals, I preferred the cockpit to remain a magical place beyond my comprehension where experts could fix any problems. If I could see the controls, they became real, levers and buttons someone like me could touch, and I began to imagine how things could go wrong. My mom, a nervous flyer, had only agreed to board a plane to support me. It's what mothers do—bundle up their nerves, pack a Xanax or two, and throw back a shot of Kahlua before takeoff. She sat to my left, and in my memory she presents as a buzz, a person with low-grade electrical impulses jumping from the outline of her body. On the flight from Columbus to Newark, New Jersey, we'd played hangman to distract ourselves. My secret sentence: I don't like flying. Unlike Mom, I didn't fear we'd crash. I feared, just as I had halfway to Spain, that my throat would close from an anaphylactic reaction and I would die before we could land. Mom, whose own heart was likely racing, assured me we could always take the bus back home. She knew just what to write. She wrote it for me, for herself.

My sister Sienna and my dad sat across the aisle. I don't remember why Autumn couldn't join us on the trip. We began our descent into Columbus, the pilot's voice drifting in through the speakers, Mom like a kid waiting for a Ferris wheel to let her off.

But after thirty minutes, we still didn't touch down. Instead, the plane lowered, then came a roar and shift, a gunning ascent, and we were back up in the air.

The signposts on any plane are the flight attendants. Everything about their movements remained calm, even as the pilot announced, "It appears there is a glitch in the computer that controls the front landing gear. We are going to descend one more time so that the control tower and people on the ground can get a look at it."

Mom emitted a soft song of hems and haws, and the attendant knelt down to hold her hand. Dad, who'd slept through the first descent, woke up and grabbed Sienna's hand. Having worked for two years as an America West ramp agent, he knew the ins and outs of planes, which noises and commands were not normal. The man behind me asked to be with the rest of his family, seated farther back. Another passenger began writing a note to his wife.

On the second descent, we came close enough to see strips of gray become highways with real cars moving like giant Chiclets between the dotted lines. I fixed my gaze through the window on the boxed houses below, the square plots of land, and thought of my friend at home watching *The Rosie O'Donnell Show*. In the worst moments of a person's life, other people are watching TV, surfing the internet, folding clothes, having sex. People engage in the utterly mundane while others slip away.

An attendant answered the phone hanging by his head. Mom could have measured the blood that drained from his face. And then followed words that didn't make sense in my head but forced my legs to move: "We need everyone to move to the back of the plane. Leave your purses and luggage. Everyone to the back of the plane in crash position."

We followed, herded like sheep, some yelling, some silent. When we reachced the back, my mother put her arm over me, as though her body could shield me from a vessel of metal crashing to the ground. To my right, Sienna looked out the window, crying. My dad, across the aisle from us, prayed with his head down, his thick thumbs clasped under his widow's peak. But I didn't want him to just pray. I wanted those hands that helped manufacture cars to hold us up, for his prayer to spin a web I could see and feel that would keep us in the air until we could safely land. I needed him to promise me with confidence, not bow himself in desperation. He'd guided me through eighth grade honors algebra by breaking down each chapter and formula, each $x$, until I could interpret the questions. All I needed now was for those same hands, that same mind, to get us to the ground in one piece.

I heard our principal's voice on the morning announcements: *As you know, your classmate Taylor Sharp was selected as a finalist in the ESPN Essay Contest this year. Unfortunately, on her way back from New York . . .*

Dad reached across and grabbed the hand of my mother, his ex-wife, the woman who'd asked him to the Sadie Hawkins dance in high school, the two of them perched on haystacks in plaid shirts and jeans in the photo. I closed my eyes. There would be a terrible drop, but I would black out, then peace. I'd be in heaven. I knew of Jesus, the one who'd been battered, wrongly convicted. I knew he had a power I couldn't understand and thought he'd recognize me enough.

Unlike Sienna, I didn't think of our sister Autumn. She'd stayed home and would be left alone. I don't know if birth order or anxiety or both caused me to think only of myself. And a bit about my mother, that she hadn't wanted to fly for fear of crashing. What's the word for when your fear is valid after all?

"In the next thirty seconds . . ." are the last words I remember from the pilot.

When a plane's front landing gear is turned ninety degrees in the wrong direction, the plane might hit the runway with locked front wheels and flip in a somersault, end over end. Ambulances gathered hundreds of feet below our feet. Autumn drove her car to the dentist. I waited for the free fall.

Instead, like a spoon skimming the top of yogurt, we landed, the pilot expertly touching the plane's back wheels to the runway first, then allowing the nose to drop and skid. "Drinks on me!" a guy in front of us shouted, and we laughed, sweet relief pouring on us like champagne.

The attendants ripped doors open on either side and filed us out. Children first! Mom pushed Sienna and me forward. Would the plane explode after we'd cheered? I was directed to the right, where I slid down an orange blow-up slide, hit the ground, and ran in the wrong direction. Where was safety? No one had said what to do after you touched the ground. An adult signaled me to come back the other way, away from an endless field of green, from what looked safe to me.

Later I found out that we were supposed to fly Continental, but Mom had switched to America West after looking up safety records. What do you call the circumstances fear can't control?

An airline employee gave us food vouchers, and the four of us sat around a table at Max & Erma's, our favorite burger joint. Sienna spilled iced tea all down her shirt. *She's really shaken up,* I thought.

A week or two later, the panic attacks caught up to me—in math class, in my living room, on the front stairs of my high school as I waited for a ride home. Every morning before school, Mom pulled up to the curb and reassured me I wouldn't die. The more she said I'd be okay, the more I needed her to say I'd be okay. When I wasn't trapped in my head, I'd try to remember what it was like to walk with friends, to laugh. My classmates, with their hiking backpacks and North Face fleeces, making plans for the weekend, living untethered. How had I once been free and then not?

My brain had been right to worry on that plane, but it continued to harvest the same level of panic long after I was safe. Rachel, the pediatric psychologist with straight brown hair and small eyes, gave me a name for the way my brain worked overtime, looking for danger.

What we're looking at here, is separation anxiety, Dr. Dawdy had told my mother.

What we're looking at here, is generalized anxiety disorder, Rachel said to me.

What we're looking at here, is failure to thrive, the endocrinologist wrote in Tophs's chart.

Do I believe my separation anxiety was tied to a deeper and broader anxiety, already threaded into my genes? I do. But a story about an infant's dehydration cannot serve as proof that a more dangerous disorder hid beneath. It's anecdotal conjecture. Maybe my body, no matter what, would have always taken sixteen years to fully declare itself as one given to fear.

Rachel was the first person I remember looking me in the eye, with clarity and warmth, to give me a diagnosis that housed all my symptoms. True, I had panic attacks, but it wasn't just panic disorder. Sure, I hated crowds, but it wasn't only agoraphobia. Who could say if or when I would fly again, but it wasn't only a fear of flying that kept me in bed. The diagnosis of generalized anxiety disorder, with symptoms of depression (especially as I cut myself off from the world in panic), gave me space. It gave me an area within a thick book called the *Diagnostic and Statistical Manual of Mental Disorders* (*DSM*) along Axis I. But it also allowed me to distance myself from terrible thoughts and patterns that had started to define me. While some people avoid labels out of concern they will be defined by a disorder, I found comfort in the naming. Rachel had seen this before, the prognosis wasn't awful, and medicine could help. She never promised the fear would vanish, but she didn't have to. She designed a treatment plan, and as my panic attacks decreased from seven to two every day and then two per week, and as I drove myself around the block or to the tennis courts and back, I learned how to recognize and disarm my fear.

The combination of Paxil, an antidepressant, and cognitive behavioral therapy felt as good as a cure most days. Even as I matured into an adult and my anxiety took new forms, I never faced a doctor or therapist who was completely puzzled by my irrational thoughts or ruminations. As much as I can despise my anxiety and dream of a life without it, I can at least always find a home in my diagnosis. I can always locate a therapist to help me brush up on strategies to combat my negative thinking. I've wanted that same home for my son.

So much about Tophs challenged the rewiring of my brain I'd worked to accomplish through therapy. If a scary automatic thought invaded, finding ways to disprove it wasn't so simple. Sometimes I found too much evidence to support it.

**Thought:** *What if his blood sugar drops too low overnight?*
**Evidence:** He once ate a high-calorie dinner of pizza and ice cream and still woke up with a blood glucose level of twenty-seven.

Even thoughts that should be easy to rule out took more effort.

**Thought:** *What if his heart suddenly stops beating?*
**Evidence:** He doesn't have a primary carnitine deficiency, so that probably won't happen. But he might have a secondary carnitine issue that was resolved through medication, and we don't know why those levels initially dropped. His levels could drop again; would that affect his heart?

The most dangerous, insidious thought took a lot of effort to unravel—

**Thought:** *What if, when he rolled off my bed as an infant, Tophs sustained brain damage?*
**Evidence:** His head was shaped differently on one side for as long as I can remember, but the doctors weren't concerned. They called it positional plagiocephaly and insisted we didn't need a shaping helmet. I couldn't understand a lot of his speech at age two, but I had gone to speech therapy as a kid, and so had Eliot. But was he understanding me? Was I getting through to him, and, if not, was it somehow my fault?

This particular concern, Me as Cause, grew and grew, and I worked hard to lessen its power. Surely the fall from the bed hadn't made him a five-pound baby. A fall doesn't make your glucose plummet twenty months later. I don't think it kicks you off the growth curve before your first birthday. In this way, I found hope in *more* things being abnormal about Tophs, because a systemic issue would likely absolve me of wrongdoing. Maybe I was strong enough to raise a son whose body and mind puzzled me. I was not strong enough to raise a son whose body and mind were puzzling *because* of me. I've never believed everything happens for a reason. But if God had designed my son and allowed him to emerge from my womb this way, I knew I could find peace and joy in mothering him. I already had. If, however, I had hurt or changed the human God had designed, my guilt would erode any peace. Nothing has ever threatened to consume me quite like this shame.

Just as Tophs's hypoglycemia and elevated AST might be True, True, and Unrelated, I began to see that his health and my anxiety disorder could be too. I could have irrational thoughts, he could have abnormalities, and his abnormalities might not be inventions of my imagination. They might not be the metaphorical equivalent of brain aneurysms I'd been so terrified of as a teenager. His medical symptoms and answer-less doctor's appointments did trigger my anxiety and depression. But I began to understand that even if Tophs had another mom, one not predisposed to irrational thoughts, he would still experience perplexing illness, not just sore throats and earaches or fixable hernias. I was his mother, not an inventor of maladies.

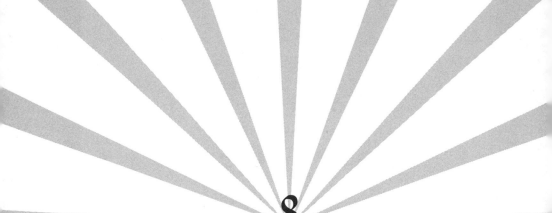

8

On his first day of preschool, Tophs grins at the camera, his head recently shaved by Paul in the bathroom, a Harris boy rite of passage. He wears the Mike Posner lifeguard outfit with the tiniest boat shoes you've ever seen. Following in his big sister's footsteps, he'll attend the cozy school housed within a Methodist church.

When we'd previously toured the preschool for Eliot, the blonde director, Paige, whose Alabama drawl thickened as she grew more comfortable, won me over. She spoke of diversity without using the buzzword, talked in such a genuine way I knew my shy, Black daughter would be seen, if not heard. At the end of Eliot's first year of preschool, Paige had returned to the public school system to teach special education, so she wouldn't be teaching Tophs. But I trusted the warm community she'd cultivated. Now the bright-eyed, pleasant baby had become the fearless two-year-old who beamed for the camera.

Tophs's teachers loved him, sending photos of him cheesing at the art table, the left dimple on full display, his smile a hundred teeth wide. "Tophs never saw a picture of himself he didn't like," his teacher joked. I had produced an easygoing, adorable ham. So different than me. I, like Eliot, had grabbed on to my mother's pants as a young child, forbidding her to leave me at kindergarten orientation. If it's true that we want what we can't have, then it's Tophs's natural ease around people that I covet, the way he high-fived college girls handing out flyers around campus. But if we want our children to have what we can't, then his ease has brought me nothing but joy.

He and Eliot attended school on alternating days. On mornings when Tophs stayed home with me, I would try to read to him. He would take the book, flip quickly through the pages, as though he'd find a prize in the back, and scream or whine if I tried to read or point at illustrations. Sometimes he would slow down, examine the pictures, and say, "Ohhhh," to himself. Maybe he was just different than Eliot, who memorized entire books, reciting them with great expression. He did seem to like learning his letters and sounds with the LeapFrog Letter Factory DVD I'd let him watch as we waited for Eliot to get out of school. Every time a teacher walked Eliot to the van and slid the door open, I wondered what they thought about this two-year-old addicted to a screen. It wasn't a Waldorf school, but Tophs refused to even look over when they greeted him. *Yep*, I thought, *they're definitely judging us.*

I tried to reach him through play. I'd pull out a carefully selected wooden puzzle or alphabet blocks, the kind I thought Moms Who Had It All Together purchased when they weren't whittling their own puzzles from birch or roasting salmon with herbs from the community garden. Tophs, though, would throw the puzzle or push it aside with a warning grunt. A few times, he became so upset that he hit his head against the thin carpet of our floor or our kitchen wall. One morning, when he refused to stack rings or blocks and just seemed mad at life, I finally texted Paul at work.

*I don't know what to do with him. It's like I can't get through.*

*I hear you. That's tough. I wonder if a schedule would help.*

Paul's answer validated me. He'd noticed, though I still wasn't sure to what extent. While Paul is a creature of good and orderly habits (I mean, the man's first suggestion was to *make a schedule)*, I'm the weird artistic one who observes and remembers. I have always struggled to create structure from chaos, and that's where Paul regularly saves the day.

He's been a planner from the beginning. Early into my third year at UVA, Paul drove from his home in Hampton to take me to dinner. He'd finished grad school and was working as a high school counselor. "I'd like you to be my girlfriend," he said, winding his way down the two-lane road to my apartment.

"Oh, really? I'll have to pray about it." I liked him. A lot. He'd visited me in Ohio over the summer. *Um, a friend doesn't drive to Ohio,* my friend said. She was right. But I'd started coming into my own as a Christian in college, right when Joshua Harris's books on courtship and purity were bible. Paired with my natural rule-following ways, I was determined to get this relationship exactly right.

"Listen, fellas," Paul's since preached in sermons, "I had no chance! She and her friends made T-shirts that read JESUS IS MY BOO."

He's not lying. But Paul kept showing up, once driving hours just to leave a rose at my door, and I kept quietly wanting to jump his bones. Still, I convinced him we should wait until marriage to kiss.

That Valentine's Day, instead of being salty that I hadn't given him a yes yet, he took me to the Rotunda before our dinner reservations at Outback. He carried a basket, and as we sat on the steps, looking out at the Lawn, he handed me several roses. Nine, one for every month since June when he'd visited me in Ohio, sleeping in my mom's basement and driving me to the outlet mall where we ate fresh kettle corn. He'd taped a slip of paper with a date to each stem, from June 2003 to February 2004, and a word. When I put them in order, they read, *Taylor, it's still fun getting to know you better.*

Then he pulled out a bottle of sparkling cider, and we laughed because he'd failed to bring a bottle opener. "Well, I'll never make that mistake again," he said, and he never has. Was there anything that couldn't be accomplished with a plan? We said we'd start trying to get pregnant five years into our marriage, and we did. Said we'd move back to Charlottesville one day, and we did. We talked around the calling on his life to preach—almost too scared to really touch it, hold it. But the day we dedicated Tophs to the Lord as an infant, at a historic Black Baptist church, Paul told me he felt ready to take the next step: seminary. I flipped out, not even in a sanctified way. Somehow knowing he'd preach one day had not prepared me for his need to prepare *now* to preach one day.

"When were you going to tell me this?!"

"That's why I'm mentioning it now. Let's talk about it. I'm not sure I want to put it off any longer."

Soon after, I called the wife of our former pastor in northern Virginia. I called her from a safe space, the Starbucks parking lot.

"There are just these expectations," I told her. I imagined myself being called First Lady and having to wear white gloves and tights with kitten heels. What if I started pouring fruit punch from those gallon jugs after service or carrying a handkerchief at all times?

"You don't have to be those things," she reassured me. "Don't let other people put those expectations on you. And don't put them on yourself." She cautioned that Paul and I would have to communicate about schedules and routines. There were only so many hours in a day, and our kids wouldn't need us any less just because we were busy.

A tight schedule is the only way Paul (and our family) survived working full-time at UVA while going to seminary an hour away on nights and weekends. *I'll make it work*, was Paul's motto. And he did—he managed to show up as a father and husband and professor and divinity student—believing God had called him to all those roles.

But even as I broke my days with Tophs into sections and made lists of activities, I couldn't quite make it work. He often flailed or resisted when it came time to transition. I was a stay-at-home mom. I had one job. No one said it should be easy. But sometimes, when I wasn't feeding or cuddling Tophs, when I wasn't changing his diaper or making silly faces, I felt that more than mothering, I was just watching. Trying to figure out ways I could join him. The right toys, the right routines weren't enough. I will never be as organized as Paul; in fact, I *need* room for spontaneous Krispy Kreme runs in my life. But I grew up with a deep belief that if I made the right choices; if I finished my homework and studied for tests; if I followed the syllabus, or the Ten Commandments, I would be more than okay. I would be a success, full stop.

I'm in fourth grade, lying on my back in bed, looking through the blinds out my window. I recount the stories my sisters and I have been told: Mom and Dad in summer school together, where Dad fell asleep in Chemistry and still got the right answer, while Mom excelled in writing. They won best couple, a silhouette of their faces in black and white in their senior yearbook. Each went on to one college, then another, a transfer here, a loss of credit hours there, a call from back home—for Mom, to return to her single mother, who didn't have any more money to send. All the forces and inertia, patterns started long before them, combined to pull them from their college campuses less than two semesters before graduation. Then a pregnancy, my eldest sister as embryo, a Reno wedding with a best man in overalls, then factory and office jobs and dreams deferred. Raising three daughters in a racist suburb, where a teacher told my sister, "Be thankful you're not at that other (mostly Black) high school." All so their girls could get the best education possible and graduate from college, so they could make good on that potential our people have been carrying for years, long before the water hoses, the Middle Passage, all the way back to when the Father molded us—yes, us *too*—from the dust and blew life into our Black bodies' lungs. Thanks be to God.

So I'm in fourth grade, and the weight of everything my parents wanted to achieve; the weight of heating up water on the stove for baths when we were late paying bills; the weight of my parents' arguments laced with regret and loss; the weight of Dad walking into that dark and steamy factory every day, the weight of Mom typing what the doctors dictated in her ear rather than her own poetry; all that weight fell from the sky, singed my skin, began to melt and reform my insides. Left spaces I thought we could fill. Even as my sisters and I earned straight As and academic scholarships and graduate degrees, I wondered if we could do enough, be enough to change the structure of the void. I'm not sure if we did, even less sure who is qualified to judge. Looking back, I realize that striving, the need to make good on my potential, did not stop after college or grad school or my first big publication. It didn't stop when I became a mother. The drive for success didn't look like a career on Wall Street, but maybe it took the form of a quiet assumption that I would, all things considered, be able to give my children whatever they needed.

While we didn't know the cause of Tophs's physical symptoms, we could at least quantify them, measure them with a quick blood draw. A body's carnitine level is low or it's not. The same with blood sugar. His AST, that pesky, nonspecific enzyme, remained slightly elevated on every test. What became harder to describe, impossible to quantify, was the disconnect I felt between us.

One afternoon Tophs woke up from a nap, and I gave him goldfish in a plastic bag. Wearing a diaper and shirt, he ran into the kitchen, threw his goldfish, and began to scream as they spread across the tile floor. He stood on his tiptoes, reached his hands up to the gray countertop, and tried to climb up the flat cabinet doors beneath.

"Tophs, what do you want? Do you want your goldfish?" Dumb questions. But the fact that he thought he could climb a flat wall, that he didn't jump up on his toes and then turn around, unsettled me. The way it still does when elementary-aged Tophs believes he can sew me a coffee machine from fabric, one that will brew real coffee.

After clawing at the counter and garbling commands, willing me to help him, then piercing me with those huge and angry eyes, he eventually gave up and fell onto the floor. Still crying, he flipped over onto his stomach and began flailing, as though swimming, smashing the fallen crackers over the cold charcoal tiles.

Eliot called for me in the background—she needed me too— needs me too—but Tophs's hoarse cry drowned her out. He stood back up and tried to climb the cabinet doors once more before settling for rubbing his hands over them, the way a toddler might rub a blanket. He had succumbed to or been soothed by something I couldn't see.

The goldfish tantrum was loud and obvious. But what could I make of the behaviors I didn't have words for? Once again, I turned to Google. There, on the screen, a young brown-skinned boy ran along the sidewalk, his eyes to the side, like I'd seen with Tophs. This was called stimming, or self-stimulation. The repetition of movements, sounds, or words. People online seemed to know about it, especially parents of children with autism. Tophs's dancing, his clapping, his stomping. The way he moved back and forth in front of a glass china cabinet at a friend's baby shower, mimicking his reflection, for too long. We had watched, laughing. Maybe it wasn't funny at all.

The image of that little Black boy both haunted and informed.

It wasn't that he had autism. For all my time spent Googling, I didn't actually know enough about autism spectrum disorder to fear it. But I saw too much white in that boy's eyes as he ran, and I wondered how often he could be reached. I wondered if the person behind the camera missed him.

Tophs also began to cry from his crib in the dark, always around 3:00 a.m. It had taken us two rounds of sleep training to get him to sleep through the night. "Maybe his circadian rhythm is off," his teacher suggested as I dropped off a sleepy Tophs one morning. I pictured cicadas, wide awake with those bulging eyes, chirping all night.

"I give my kids melatonin gummies," a mom friend confessed. But I worried about putting anything into Tophs's system that might add another unknown to the list. So I woke up, carried him down the hall to the living room, where he wiggled out of my arms and stood in front of the computer, crying and pointing.

"Wan' watch? Watch!" he said, asking for music videos.

"No, Tophs. It's nighttime. It's not time to watch." He cried, and sometimes I gave in. But one night I held him in my arms on the couch, with every light out, except for the lasers moving across the screensaver. He looked back at me, calm, unblinking eyes too wide and too white; their focus unnerved me.

Suddenly, the memory of that perfect day marked by peace as I climbed the stairs with him surfaced, this time dipped in dread. What if I wouldn't lose him physically but instead lose him behind the shield of those eyes?

"Tell me what you're most concerned about," Dr. Quillian asked at his next appointment.

She wanted my deepest fear, and I quickly searched for a way out before relenting. "I read about Smith-Magenis. I'm not sure how you pronounce it."

Children with the syndrome might flip quickly through books, stay up at night, have a hoarse voice, short stature, and reduced sensitivity to pain. They often had temper tantrums that could include head banging, but also had "affectionate, engaging personalities."

"Oh, no. I can tell you for sure he doesn't have that. I have patients with that, and Tophs just doesn't fit."

Earlier in Tophs's life, I might have felt shame that I'd jumped to the wrong conclusion. But that day, Dr. Quillian's absolute certainty brought relief, much like the test results of my youth. We could cross one more diagnosis off the list.

Growing up, no one cared for me the way Mom did when I was sick. She'd hammer ice cubes tucked into a pillowcase on the kitchen counter so that I could suck on small shards until my stomach settled. If my legs ached, she brought a heating pad. If my nose was stuffy, she handed me a medicine spoon filled with minty green liquid. Most tests came back negative, but if I did have strep throat, she talked me down before the big shot of antibiotic; if it was pink eye, she let me relax on the couch and read. When I nearly fainted from menstrual cramps, she picked up a prescription so that I could sleep them off. Even when the pain was more emotional, like when I didn't test into the gifted program my big sisters had, she somehow made me believe I was just as smart. The next time I took the test, I got in.

Nothing threatened this superpower of hers like my anxiety disorder. She could identify with fear, the kind she experienced on planes and freeways, but the way I'd crumbled in Spain, the aftershock of the emergency plane landing, how I would suffer a breakdown before my last semester of college—the depth and breadth of my anxiety is quite possibly unmatched within my family tree. My sisters have faced their own physical and emotional challenges, the stories theirs to tell, but *fear*, the constant and crippling kind, belongs to me.

I've never asked my mother, "What do you do when the illness you thought was *temporary* turns out to be an integral part of your child's makeup? When you can't ever cross it off a list?"

You take an understood oath as a parent not to compare your child—to other kids on the playground or to their siblings. With kids, we use "objective" milestones. But show me a mother who doesn't notice that her first child hit a particular milestone and her second did not. She doesn't forget the distance between the two, or the three, though she doesn't divide her love accordingly either.

Memory shifts and recedes over time, and I remembered Eliot talking later than her peers. When Tophs spoke gibberish, I saw him as following in her footsteps. But I had misremembered. Eliot may have taken longer to speak and done so with a slight stutter, she may have even been the shyest kid in the room, but she and I held conversations. We shared a verbal give-and-take. How had I missed this?

In a video taken when she was two, she stands in front of me on foam letters to read me a simple board book. She labels toothbrushes, berries, boots, and "gasses" for glasses.

"What color are those glasses?" I ask.

"Blue."

It's simple, but dangerous, this clip. It both confirms my sense about Tophs and punctures my sense of normalcy and control. The cut of this double-edged sword is long and deep. Whenever a test result or a teacher's observation confirms what I've known, I breathe easy. *I was right. I'm not making this up.* Then I take a moment, look down, and realize I'm bleeding out. I'm gutted by a video I filmed when he was about two and a half:

Tophs sits on a beige swivel chair by the computer, dressed in striped cotton pants and a long-sleeved shirt, the kind of cozy outfit I loved to buy at the Gap in Richmond after we'd dropped Paul off down the road at seminary. He's eating a Jolly Rancher popsicle.

"What are you doin', Tophs?" I ask. Those eyes, so much pupil, find me.

"Un-uh," he says, his lips closed, chewing. He's almost smirking.

"What are you eating?"

He looks at me, starts to shake his head, then tilts it to the side and raises his eyebrows.

"Huh?" I ask. He tosses his head back against the chair. "Are you eating a popsicle?"

He looks down, takes a bite, and says, "Uh . . . coco," and looks at me.

"Popsicle?"

"No." He shakes his head.

"No? What is it?"

"No." He shakes his head again.

"Huh?"

"Ido-sicle," he suggests, shrugging his shoulders and gesturing with his empty hand.

"It's a sicle, yeah, pop-sicle."

"Ino-sicle," he points toward me.

"How is it?"

"Ino-sicle. *Si-kol*," as though he's carefully showing me how to say it.

"Sicle? Pop-si-cle. Good boy."

"Ino-sicle. Ohhh. Whoa." He looks down at the popsicle, as though he's just realized something new.

"What?"

"In-i-mo-sicle."

"How does it taste?"

"Uhhh . . . sicle-anmi?" he asks himself and looks out the corner of his eyes. "Yes," he answers.

These were conversations with Tophs. This was the boy I loved more than myself. This was the distance that started small—a cloud the size of a man's hand rising from the sea—and grew until it nearly ripped me in half.

9

Tophs loved morning circle time at school—the dancing and singing—but when it came time to answer a question, he didn't speak. His teachers, discerning that he wanted extra fruit or crackers at snack time, taught him the sign for *more*, and he came home, happily touching his fingers and thumbs together in our kitchen.

He made friends too. My friend Erin's daughter, Coco, became his favorite. We set up a lunch date for the four of us at Bodo's, a popular Charlottesville bagel shop. We found a table with chairs on one side and a booth on the other near the large windows. As Erin sorted the orders—a sesame bagel with butter for Coco, a plain bagel with butter for Tophs—Coco grew impatient, pulling at Erin. "I'm hungry," she whined.

*She's hungry? She's hungry! She's two and she's hungry and she's telling her mom.* Tophs had never said he was hungry. At home, he'd sign and say "mo nack" for snack or point to a box of crackers

on the counter or to the refrigerator for milk, but he never expressed hunger or thirst. What else was I missing?

"I've never heard him say that."

Erin looked up, her eyes taking in my face, likely noticing the
shift in my tone, but I could tell she didn't know what to make of
my emphasis on this fact. She and I had connected over the shyness
of our firstborns and, to her, Tophs was a silly and lovely boy who
danced a lot. I unwrapped his bagel from the wax paper, and he
ate and drank just like his friend Coco. I knew then, even to sweet
Erin, who was always a safe place to land with my parenting wor-
ries, this absence of words from Tophs couldn't signal to her what
it did to me. Another clear and painful yardstick. A terrible and
beautiful affirmation.

That winter of Tophs's first year of preschool, Dr. Quillian
wrote, *I remain concerned about Christopher.* His blood count always showed excess here or a low number there, and twice "tear-
drop" cells had been noted, without any explanation by the lab.
The big tests, like the chromosomal microarray, which searched
for extra or missing sections of chromosomes, came back normal. But so many others returned with numbers highlighted in
yellow. Dr. Quillian referred us to a developmental pediatrician,
who had a long waitlist, and sent us for a speech and language
evaluation.

Anita, our new speech pathologist, greeted us in the waiting
area of the UVA Children's Hospital, and Tophs eagerly followed
her down the hallway, bouncing and bubbling over with Tophs-
ness. He loved Anita's room—toys tucked into bins, a blue gym-
nastics mat, a wooden chair at a desk alongside a wide mirror where
he could stare at himself. He played as I gave her some history: the

words I hadn't heard, the ways I couldn't connect. She jotted down notes, switching her gaze from me to him, then back to me.

"You're not worried he has autism, are you?"

"I don't know what he has." Maybe she thought I was *that* mom. My child had been a little slow to talk, and I had jumped straight to autism. Maybe she'd seen a lot of those moms, but I wasn't one of them. Unless, of course, we are all that mom sometimes.

Tophs sat in that wooden highchair, and she gave him a red lollipop. He happily watched himself bite it in the mirror, but when she directed him to open his mouth or show his tongue, he didn't respond. He didn't imitate her. I prompted him, trying not to jump in too early. She asked him for scissors. Nothing. She asked again, this time visually prompting him with her hands, and then he handed them over.

He said a few words clearly, like *purple, circle,* and *monkey,* but apropos of nothing; he seemed to just like these words. Maybe Coco had become his best friend because he liked the sound of her name. He also said *ya* often, as though he was following the conversation, along with a lot of jargon neither of us could decipher. But then he counted to ten. He even knew some of his letters and sounds, courtesy of LeapFrog's Professor Quigley.

When Anita asked him *wh-* questions, he echoed her. She was bent over, shifting between studying him and writing down notes and sounds he made on a formal assessment. Then she turned to me. "Well, he's befuddling."

Left hook. The punch landed, then caressed. *You're onto something, Mom.* Anita's evaluation read: *It was difficult to obtain specific age ranges for speech and language abilities because Christopher's abilities were so scattered.*

She had observed enough to diagnose him with a receptive and expressive speech delay. The receptive aspect referred to what he understood, the expressive to what he could say. He wasn't Tophs to Anita yet, but he would be soon enough. We'd visit Anita every week on the fourth floor of the hospital, first alone and then paired with Liz, an occupational therapist. The two worked in tandem, spinning Tophs in a swing, teaching him words, strengthening his small hands with a magnetic fishing game, and giving me ideas for how to engage him at home.

"Okay, Christopher," Anita would prompt. "How do we make the car go? One, two, three . . . What do you say? One, two, three? *Go!*"

"Go!"

She rewarded him by pushing a button on top of a car and letting it speed away. In the moments when he didn't respond, when she didn't push the car without a *go* from him, I learned to swallow the burn in my stomach. It was okay to show a little tough love; he wouldn't collapse, not from this.

Tophs loved movement: the push-and-go car, the square-shaped swing hooked to the ceiling, the room covered in padded blocks and cylinders he could climb through. He'd find a mat and bend down, putting weight on his head. I smiled, never worried, but Anita would squirm in the corner. "Oh no, I'm not good with this," she'd say, concerned for his neck. For me, it was never the possibility of a broken bone or cut or sprain that made me nervous for Tophs. It was all the things we couldn't see.

Anxiety, a wind, is known by what it moves. By the people and objects it knocks down or holds hostage, those it unhinges without permission. When my parents unpacked our minivan on move-in day at UVA, they knew the ways in which the school would be a good fit for me. I mean as much as a predominantly white, southern institution built by slaves can fit a Black student. What I didn't ask them was if they thought I'd make it. If the Paxil and therapy with Rachel had been enough.

Sure, they cared whether we'd purchased the right meal plan and textbooks, but even with my sister Autumn studying across Grounds at UVA Law, did they assume they'd be driving back in the middle of the night that semester to pick me up? Not because I'd drank too much or failed midterms or broken up with my first college boy, but because the chalkboards of the lecture halls had started closing in, or the dining hall food got stuck in my throat, or the bus ride to student health would take too long in case of an emergency.

It's only now that I'm curious what it took for my parents to drive away from my dorm, seeing what others couldn't see in me. If anxiety is my body's disproportionate response to risk, how did my parents determine what would be an appropriate level of risk for me? For them? Really, how does any parent live each day without knowing their child will be safe, will land on their feet?

"There he goes again," Anita would say as Tophs turned upside down, his head pressed against the floor. "Liz, this is your area."

Liz would walk over and stand next to him, like a spotter. "He definitely seems to like that pressure on his head," she said, "and that crash-and-bang type of play. Do you guys have a beanbag at home? Or what about one of those mini trampolines he could jump on?"

Finally, the internet became my friend. I shopped for a bargain, and soon we owned a blue exercise trampoline. As I unpacked the box, I made sure to speak slowly and loudly so that Paul, who was Marie Kondo before Marie Kondo, could hear: "Liz and Anita, from the *hos-pi-tal* recommended this. I'll put it over here in the *cor-ner* for him. It's practically invisible if you don't look."

Taking Tophs to see Anita and Liz every week felt like tangible progress. Liz noted his fine motor delay—how the size of his hands made grasping objects difficult—and paid attention to his sensory needs in order to figure out what made him tick. The hope was that as Liz gave Tophs the sensory input he needed, Anita's speech lessons would have the maximum impact. We had a dream team of professional women who worked well together, who shifted their schedules to accommodate Tophs because they believed that would be best for him. This is the sort of out-of-the-box thinking I'd long for later in some IEP meetings when bureaucracy ruled the day, to the detriment of my son.

Liz and Anita couldn't explain why Tophs had the strengths and weaknesses he did, but their goals were measurable, and they knew him. They sat with him week after week and learned he wouldn't touch shaving cream or that he chewed his shirt when nervous or paid attention longer if he could take jumping breaks.

On the best days, which could still be sad days for me, Anita and Liz sat at the bottom of that pool I'd dreamed of, right next to my boy. If he gazed straight ahead, if he turned without warning, if he tucked his head under for a somersault instead of coming up for air, they stayed. If he sucked in water instead of blowing out bubbles, they patted his back and took note. They could not be his

mother, they could not be God, they could not be the Great Doctor with the Big Answer, but they could be present and curious.
They could show up with open hands, without fear of what they
couldn't do.

10

Leaving Ohio to attend UVA turned out to be worth the risk—but not just because I proved to my parents or myself that I could live on my own. It's where I met the other Blacks.

In my hometown of Bexley, a suburb of Columbus, when two of us took the same AP class, the teacher confused our names. I'd never even had a Black teacher outside of a middle school home-room teacher who marked me present. So when I first walked Jefferson's Grounds, instead of seeing a modern-day plantation, I saw a version of *A Different World*'s Hillman College. We were an entire 10 percent of the student population!

I learned the unwritten rules quickly. Black students generally greeted each other, and we ate at the same time in one section of the dining hall. We also hung out at a particular bus stop between classes. We didn't need white people the way I'd needed them all my life. We could befriend them, but they didn't make our sun rise.

The frat boys could wear their orange bow ties and blue blazers, swoop their swoopy hair to the side, and no one bothered them, but when they walked past the Black bus stop, it was clear who ran the stoop.

This way of being, this freedom from panic and freedom from whiteness, defined my first year at UVA. When my roommate turned to me midsemester and said, "I've never known a Black girl who didn't wear big hoop earrings and have an attitude," I told her that was foolish and kept it moving. I had nothing left to prove to whites.

What has remained with me since college is a contempt for racism and a strong love for my people. We are exceptional and beautiful, even under the weight of oppression. What's crept back in from my childhood is a subtle deference to whites in some public spaces, and not just those who carry guns and wear badges. There's still a part of me that is a ten-year-old girl surrounded by Black people in church but looking at the white visitors, hoping *they'll* feel comfortable. I doubt that girl completely disappeared in college, but I needed her less. It's not only with white people. Put me in front of Oprah and see how I act. But it's that I slip into the role, invite the little girl back so quickly, with people who might not hate me but might be indifferent to my and my family's well-being. That's the part of me I want to cancel.

In March, two months before Tophs turned three, he awoke vomiting water, that weary and vacant look on his face. He let me prick his finger without a fight. The glucometer read forty-eight. Paul and I had been waiting for this. Hoping nothing serious would happen but ready to drive straight to the ER for critical labs if Tophs's glucose dropped below sixty. The endocrinologist had printed out a letter with her signature and all the tests she wanted run while his glucose remained low. I carried the letter in my purse; Paul had taken a picture of it and emailed it to both of us, just in case. My adrenaline surged. We'd get the information the doctors needed. I texted Dr. Quillian on our way, and she called ahead to the ER for us.

They took us back right away, and I even recognized the nurse with the ponytail. "You helped us last time this happened," I said, trying to make a connection. I handed over the list of tests printed on UVA letterhead.

The nurse poked Tophs's finger with the hospital-grade glucometer, and the bustling stopped. "Well, his blood sugar is sixty right now, which is normal. Do you want me to give him a popsicle?"

I backpedaled. *It must have been me. User error.* "Oh, maybe I made a mistake. It was my first time checking it in a while."

Paul spoke up. "Let's hold off on the popsicle." Thank God for Paul. I would have taken the flavor-ice pop, put my tail between my legs, and paid the $100 co-pay. But Paul was right. Even if Tophs's blood sugar was exactly sixty in that moment, he was on the edge, and anything under sixty required bloodwork. He'd vomited water less than an hour before. He had a strange and complicated medical history. Should we think for a moment before filling him with corn syrup and sending him home?

It hadn't happened yet, but today I think of Serena Williams, postpartum, halfway to death, begging the doctors to test her and treat her for a pulmonary embolism. I think about how one person, racist or not, sleepy or not, thorough or not, can act as a play-ending foil. In Tophs's case, a nurse who checked his blood sugar once using one glucometer incorrectly judged that her test should take priority over mine. In Serena's, no one cared that she was the Greatest of All Time. It's dangerous to be Black and sick. Dangerous to be Black and in need. The patient's narrative is essential for any patient, but especially a Black patient, and especially if the doctor actually listens.

The resident working that morning did. She looked at Tophs's medical history, the list of critical tests, and ordered his blood to be drawn. "No popsicle, not yet," she said. A nurse tried to collect his urine in a bag, to no avail, right as someone brought word from the lab downstairs: His blood glucose level was forty-six. We needed to get his urine as soon as possible and start the dextrose IV drip. If a kid hangs out in low-glucose land too long, you risk seizures and brain damage.

The pace picked back up, with two nurses in the room, all eyes on me. "Okay, you can put the catheter in." I'd resisted at first, hoping now that he was a year older, we'd catch his urine without it, but thirty minutes had passed, and getting our boy stable became priority. We'd moved from barely being noticed to being rushed.

Tophs did get his popsicle that day, two in fact, before discharge. Those critical lab results showed some abnormalities, but the follow-up bloodwork was normal. Tophs's results consistently showed us everything his blood could give us and yet told us little about what we could expect. His blood couldn't tell us that in two more weeks, his glucose would drop once again to forty-six, and we would race first into our kitchen, then Paul to the corner store, looking for popsicles, candy, anything with sugar.

*Why didn't we have sugar?* And why couldn't Tophs's blood hold sugar?

As one doctor explained to us, sugar is stored in the liver as glycogen. The liver breaks down glycogen and releases it into the blood when it's needed. Because the liver works as a regulating storehouse, a toddler can usually go between fourteen and twenty-four hours without eating and still maintain a normal blood glucose level. But what happens when glycogen is depleted too quickly—even when the toddler has eaten a carb-loaded bedtime snack, even when he has fasted fewer than twelve hours? It wasn't so much that Tophs's liver couldn't hold sugar. The problem seemed to be his body burned it too quickly. But *why?* And was this related to his language delay? Had running low on glucose, maybe even more times than we'd noticed, changed the way his brain processed information? Or was there a black box buried within him that contained the key to running all his systems without a hitch?

I knew the developmental pediatrician could find the box if it existed. I tried not to think about the upcoming appointment, but I felt my body and expectations gearing up for the big day. This doctor, whose wait list could wrap around our college town twice, studied kids' minds *and* bodies. Who better to understand Tophs? Dr. Quillian had messaged him and gotten us a date right before Tophs's third birthday. Before I married Paul, I prayed that the rapture wouldn't happen until I lost my virginity. *I know.* But I felt the same urgency and longing about this appointment.

While we waited, results and referrals rolled in. His endocrinologist suggested a hematologist, the gastroenterologist directed us to the geneticist, and the bloodwork still broadly supported a diagnosis of ketotic hypoglycemia.


I ran into the grocery store one afternoon while Paul waited in the van with the kids. As I neared the frozen food section, Paige, Eliot's first preschool teacher, pushed her cart around the corner. I hadn't seen her in months and still lamented Tophs's introduction to school hadn't included her.

"Heeeey! How are you?" Her twang seeped through. I tried to stand there in her presence, the kind that traps you in kindness, without crying. I shifted, pointing to the cake in her cart, a huge pastel sheet cake with thick flowers of frosting. "Oh, this is for a sweet old lady at the church."

I wasn't aware, until I saw Paige's face, how weighed down I'd felt by all of Tophs's appointments. She hadn't even asked, "Tell me what brings you in today," but that's the question I'd learned to answer. I rattled off the specialists and results in a nonlinear ambush. I can always feel when I'm carrying too much, holding too much of his body in mine. The tears gathering behind my lymph nodes—suddenly I swallowed knots—were there because I wanted this beautiful boy to be okay. I still don't know what *okay* means, but just because it's hard to pin down or define doesn't mean I don't wake up most mornings staring at its amorphous face.

Paige emailed that night: *I meant what I said about coming to take a look at Tophs. I could do a quick developmental screen—I do them all the time!*

I took Tophs to her classroom soon after. He looked around the room full of neatly stored blocks, cozy corners, and bright plastic chairs and headed straight to the sensory table, filled with tiny things he could touch and hold that wouldn't leave him sticky or wet. Paige gave him space to explore before kneeling down and talking to him, taking notes as he played.

That day, and for years to come, I wanted to ask Paige, "Have you ever seen another kid like him? Tell me if there's another. Tell me if he's alone."

Instead, I tried to stay present but out of the way, until Paige said a word that, once it came into our lives, would never quite leave. *Processing.*

It was in the way Tophs silently stared at a picture of a giraffe on a flashcard. "I could tell he knew what it was," Paige explained, "but he couldn't find the word." Processing was a catchall that wasn't a cop-out or trendy buzzword, but it proved difficult to measure, especially in a preschooler.

The very word demanded someone answer: How does a brain work? And how does a typical brain work? And who is typical?

I envisioned a neon outline of Tophs's brain against a dark screen, a Lite Brite with all the pathways aglow. As a word or thought or image entered, where did it go? How did it connect? Was there a traffic jam in one lobe, a detour that took longer but was just as safe as the original route? Had two wires been cut and then grown together in an advantageous way? Is that why he could watch a LeapFrog DVD and then recite his letters and sounds?

"Don't be afraid to double-dip," Paige advised. We could take Tophs to speech and occupational therapy at the hospital through our insurance and also have him tested by the school system to receive services for free. *Early intervention*, she said. Even if he couldn't find the words now, if we doubled down at age two, he might catch up to his peers. It was like a constitutional growth delay of his mind. *Phase-shifted* was a term I'd heard Dr. Quillian use, one I innately understood. I imagined cutting out areas of his growth charts, speech evaluations, and fine motor assessments and moving them forward over time. His progress might be a little more cut-and-paste, a little choppier than the next kid's, but who cared as long as they both ended up in the same place at high school graduation?

Looking back, I want to tell that fourth-grade girl she's doing a heck of a job. The straight As, the ambition, will help her earn a full scholarship to college, where she'll find her people and the love of her life. But I also want to warn her, to take her hand and tell her she can't fill the void by collecting achievements, gathering them like gems, clutching them to her chest. They will vaporize. They're not meaningless, no, just aren't made to fill us. But that day, when I met with Paige, I was still holding on to a map of ambition, milestones, and success I'd drawn in childhood.

My friend's daughter, who was born extremely premature, spent many days in the NICU, and her motor and speech skills lagged at first. But by the time she was two or three, no one could tell her apart from the full-term kids in her class. That was a good story. Maybe I even identified it as Christian somewhere in the depths of my mind, molded by my impression of Jesus as one who likes hard work and victory as much as grace. Never mind the Garden of Gethsemane or the night the Lord's mother watched him perish before her eyes. The story I wanted was: Boy has a tough start, boy's parents pray and work hard, boy catches up and wins in the end. We all win in the end, and the mother's anxiety is finally laid to rest. She has overcome, thanks be to God.

This plan did not include Tophs's placement in a special education classroom. I came from a loving family where your ability to finally exhale and feel proud was linked to degrees. I expected my own children to follow suit—like begets like, a seed produces fruit after its kind. My children, even if straddled with a legacy of anxiety, would be high achieving in the way of test scores.

When, after several weeks of working with Tophs, Liz and Anita strongly suggested we consider enrolling Tophs in public preschool, where he could have speech and occupational therapy regularly, it didn't click. I understood *early intervention*. I understood *help*. I didn't understand *special education*. Who was included, and would he stay there forever? Were special education classrooms an island within a school? And what did it mean for a child to need more help, whether or not it was his mother's fault? I wish I could say I received their suggestion as anything other than a letdown or evidence of personal failure.

Because I live as though credit cards are just generous debit cards, Paul scheduled an appointment for us to meet with a life insurance agent. As we sat in a bland boardroom with large windows, she asked questions about our children and warned us that Tophs might not qualify for the highest level of coverage. She presented three levels, named after superheroes, which seemed absurd. As though health challenges rendered a person less powerful or deserving of praise. But what I remember most from that meeting was the talk the agent and I shared, mother to mother, on our way out of the room. Her son, a few years older than Tophs, also struggled with delays, his name somewhere on that long list to see the same developmental pediatrician.

"It takes so long to get in," she said as we moved toward the elevator. I didn't dare mention our pediatrician had gotten our appointment bumped up. "I hope everything works out for your little guy."

"Thanks. I just can't wait to finally get some answers."

We entered that doctor's appointment as a family. While we wore regular clothes, I felt like a mom preparing everyone for picture day. Was the diaper bag packed? Did Tophs have snacks for the wait? Would Eliot be a help or a distraction as the doctor assessed Tophs? With Paul there, at least I had options if Eliot needed a break. I could relax a little. But Tophs hadn't napped well that afternoon and was in no mood to please the first doctor who entered the room, a department fellow, who would perform the first round of tests.

What she couldn't read in his medical records, we told her: "Difficulty with *wh-* questions. Hard to engage in conversation. Seems best at memorizing songs or things he's taken in visually."

We had evidence from his preschool teachers, too, who had noticed more as the year progressed: "Doesn't interact with peers at school, will occasionally play with a nonverbal student in his class. Gets frustrated when he can't communicate clearly." But it wasn't all delayed, all what he couldn't do. "Likes to cuddle, engages with family, makes good eye contact."

The fellow, as lovely as she was, stood between us and Dr. Perry, the developmental pediatrician we'd come to see. How much should we tell her? Would we have to repeat it all? Did she know how to assess him? When you wait months for an appointment, longer for answers, you need everything to go perfectly. So what I remember most about Tophs's time with the fellow is what he couldn't, or refused, to do. I both wanted him to struggle enough for her to get an accurate picture and nail the tests I knew he could, like stacking blocks. When he stacked only three or four on the table, I wanted to jump in and regulate. He could easily stack ten.

But if I said, "He usually stacks more," I'd be the mom who cares about performance over everything. So I let her prompt him when she wanted, let Tophs refuse when he wanted, hoping he wasn't the first kid they'd seen who'd missed a nap.

When Dr. Perry entered, wearing slacks and a button-down, he carried a small black case that resembled a mini backgammon board. Somehow I believed everything we'd need was packed inside. He sat down, opened the case, and asked Tophs to put the various pieces into place. In the notes, he wrote that Tophs could "reverse the form board."

I can't remember exactly what he grabbed next—was it a plain piece of white paper or a small dry erase board—and, thankfully, I didn't know the gravity of the test until it was over. He drew a horizontal line. "Can you draw this for me?" he asked. Tophs did. Then he drew a vertical line. "How about this?" Tophs's lines were shakier, fainter, made with a fisted grip, but they were there.

"Well, that's good news," Dr. Perry said. "The fact that he was able to copy those lines means his intelligence is at least on the low side of average."

Had he just handed us a life vest or shot a hole through our boat?

He finished examining Tophs in about ten minutes and then sat Paul and me down while Tophs and Eliot played. "When I look at his records—the poor growth, carnitine deficiency, history of hypoglycemia, and now global developmental delay—he's got *something*. We're just not smart enough to figure it out yet."

*Something. Global. Yet.* This wasn't a fluke. Tophs had stumped the best. I processed this much before the tunnel started to narrow.

"Given your levels of education, he's certainly an outlier."

*Outlier. Like begets like. Each seed after its own kind.*

"I think he should see Genetics again for whole exome sequencing. And he should have every new wave of genetic testing that becomes available. Science is moving so fast, and what we don't know now we might know in ten years. Maybe one day somebody in Europe will discover the Christopher syndrome."

*Every new test. Europe. My boy as a syndrome.*

And then, as the conversation wound down, "If he were my son, I'd go ahead and schedule a brain MRI."

*What will they find?*

As I sat across from Dr. Perry, I heard "outlier" as a painful marker of deficit. What did it mean that our son looked small but fine on the outside yet was struggling to communicate, to understand? What if he was lonely or frustrated or scared and couldn't tell us? What if the world was closed off to him in ways it remained wide open to me? This type of limitation was not what I'd imagined for my child. And the painful path between mystery and atypical, which was really no path at all, was not the one I thought I'd travel.

The first time I heard the term *liminal*, I was eighteen, sitting in an African American Studies 101 class at the University of Virginia. A tall and slender Professor Penningroth, his complexion like my mother's relatives, had written the words *Middle Passage* in the center of a black chalkboard. He walked us through not just the number of Black bodies taken or the number of years over which they were stolen, but what it might have been like to be yanked into a void. To live (or die) between *what was* and *what would be.*

The concept felt close and easy, like something I'd always

known. The idea of a space without bounds that held within its hull the power to harm or to free or to form—that idea has never completely left me. Would I have thought as an undergrad that liminality might one day describe some of my experiences as a Black woman in America? Yes. Would I have guessed liminality might describe my future experiences as a mother, wading through waters of science and faith, in search of the truest way to know my son? Not at all. And yet here we were, drifting from the shore of one unknown to the next. Caught somewhere between "no longer" and "not yet." It was getting harder to discern where the journey had begun and where, if ever, it would end. It was getting harder to see what, if anything, was being formed in Tophs, in me, or in us as a family through this search for answers.

When Tophs was born, I knew the justice system might unjustly place limits on him one day. Limits from the outside, from racist seeds that grew slavery and Jim Crow and the verdicts for the Central Park Five—those, while horrific, made some sense to me. Even limits from within, if they looked like anxiety or depression—illnesses that ran through many families, including my own—would not have surprised me. But the idea that wrapped within this boy I'd grown in my womb might be wrinkled genes that would make life harder for him? No, not that.

*Liminal* comes from the Latin word for *threshold*. When your life, your customs, your expectations are ripped away, as in the case of slaves, or if they disintegrate through grief and mystery, you stand at this threshold. On one side, I see the disintegration of my assumptions about myself, motherhood, my children. In the space between, the space of not yet, I tread water while going to doctor's appointments and Googling, while noticing illnesses or quirks or developmental delays, while waiting for the one doctor on the right ship to come scoop us up from the depths. On the other side, who knows? I'd always assumed the other side was an answer, a new set of boundaries, a new territory to navigate and accept. I'm not sure I would know the other side now if it slapped me in the face. How do you recognize the thing you're looking for when it has no name, no shape? *Some-day-some-one-in-Europe* . . .

This space can be relentless in its power to hold my imagination captive, to dash what's beautiful and true to pieces. Because as I sit across from the doctor and hear "outlier," as I push off into the deep, I do not think about the way Tophs wakes up early one morning to put together a puzzle all by himself. Nor how he intuitively cups my face in his hands and gazes into my eyes. I cannot yet know he is capable of ordering a metal yo-yo off Amazon without any instruction. Because Tophs will think about and do things we would never think of or be able to do at such a young age—or ever. *Outlier.*

Somehow, these truths deserve to make it to the other side, even if my hands are heavy with doubt. Moses instructed the Israelites to remember the words of the God who had delivered them from slavery: "Impress them on your children. Talk about them when you sit at home and when you walk along the road, when you lie down and when you get up. *Tie them as symbols on your hands and bind them on your foreheads.* Write them on the doorframes of your houses and on your gates."

If the great doctor never comes along in his great boat, if I never get to the other side with newly hewn doorposts, I want someone to find me. I want them to see every dream for Tophs stamped across my forehead, the names of his gifts written on my forearms.

## 12

Paul and I haven't always talked after Tophs's medical appointments. I guess neither of us got a copy of a marriage de-
votional called *Walking Together Through the Unknown*. After
heavy news, I tend to go numb, then turn inward with existential
thoughts, whereas Paul hops over to another box in his mind and
does the work in front of him. A profile written on me as Tophs's
mother would be titled "Woman Drifts Alone at Sea with Bag of
Red Velvet Donuts." Paul's would read "Man Gets Inbox Down
to Seven."

There was a time, before marriage, before parenthood, and before we faced any real problems together, when my feelings for Paul
overtook my fear of vulnerability. The summer before my last year
at UVA, I stayed in Charlottesville. I can't describe what came over
me, but I began calling my mom on the way to class every day:
"Good morning. I want to marry Paul."

"Well, maybe you guys can live in the same city for a while after you graduate."

"No, I don't think you understand. I cannot wait to marry him."

My poor mother. I harassed her in this way, as though drunk off the sunlight of Charlottesville and Paul in the summertime. She must have worried that I would lose myself in this older man with big ambitions, named after a man with ambition of biblical proportions. And maybe I was falling a little too fast, too hard, especially after stalling the whole process.

That summer I wrote in my journal: *Paul isn't in love with me. He loves me a lot, he says. He thinks "in love" means you are ready to get married or some hogwash like that. Since he didn't say he was in love with me, I pretended I wasn't in love with him. It's okay— Tamika says if he wasn't in love with me his behind wouldn't drive all the way here to see me every other weekend.*

Soon after, Paul and I sat across from each other in a booth at Ruby Tuesday. Like a twelve-year-old, I ordered buffalo chicken tenders, fries, and a soda.

"I just don't want to be falling by myself," I said.

"What if I told you we were falling together?"


In the days after we saw the developmental pediatrician, a sludge entrapped my legs, and I didn't say a word. It made walking, even to the kitchen or couch, a chore. I couldn't shower it off, couldn't sleep it off. I've learned now, after several years of being Tophs's mother, that I have to wait it out. Though I've never been di-agnosed with clinical depression, my body processes sadness in a way that makes driving or doing laundry or talking difficult. The litmus test—whether I'm just tired or the transient depression has arrived like a fever—is always a good book. If I have no desire to read, if I'm convinced there's never been a good book, or the *right* book for me, written in all the history of the world, I'm not well.

My boy had something, but Dr. Perry couldn't tell us what. I had anticipated knowing everything I needed to know about Tophs's health by 5:00 p.m. that day. For better or worse, we would know. We would have a name, not just a partial diagnosis or symptom, like hypoglycemia or receptive language disorder. We would have the black box. I can look back now and remark, "I still didn't see a pattern forming?" but I honestly had no plan for returning home without an answer. When Tophs's body ran low on glucose, his body turned to burning fat, and ketones filled his urine. When my body ran low on hope, it turned to a form of despair, clothed in apathy, and my limbs filled with lead.

But I had to keep going. Not in a CNN Hero, pat-on-the-back way. I had to keep living in the middle. Cooking Annie's Mac & Cheese for the kids; playing worship music as they danced, arms in the air; walking Tophs to the picnic table at the bottom of a hill, where he loved to jump from the top to the grass beneath.

The two of us would walk along the student gardens, up and down small sets of concrete stairs, and over to the green space between hills perfect for late-night collegiate sledding. He'd climb up by himself, first onto the wooden bench, then from the bench to the picnic table top. I would just watch, no matter that I was there. This wasn't about me, though I wondered if the distance was too great, if he could break one of those skinny shins. He'd walk to one end, like a trained diver, lining up his Velcro Pumas, then bend his knees in straight-leg jeans. He'd squat there, sometimes bouncing, as he collected his nerve and considered the drop. But always, he lifted off. I have a shot of him like this, flying, his arms stretched behind his back, curls covering his head, eyelashes long and dark, cheeks full, lips puckered as he looks down. A boy flying in his hoodie. With his legs bent at forty-five degrees, he hangs, for one piece of one second, far above his shadow, a slender and distorted version of himself that never leaves the ground.

Here we were, the two of us. One of us flying. The other not quite grounded, trying to make a worthy life in this liminal space of limited knowledge and unlimited unknown. He had always been my son, had always been himself. It was my job to let him be, to *help* him be, to strip the world apart like a papier-mâché globe and build it back up again by the time his feet landed.

Who is this boy Paul and I made? At age three, he was skinny legs tucked into Velcro shoes, the owner of a dimple I could hide in, the boy whose bed I crawled toward in the middle of the night in order to press my face into the floor at his side and pray. He still makes me remember the fragility of our bodies today. And God, how he presses his face into us, unafraid of our breath, tears, and dust. If God is the one who was, and is, and is to come, then he knows all too well the betwixt and between. It does not mean he will arrive in the big boat with the doctors and save me, save Tophs, but it means he is not merely a distant icon of the past or future.

The Jesus I grew up with, made mostly of plaster or stone, stood about eighteen inches on a ledge in the corner of my grand-mother's house and also high up near the stained-glass windows of our church in various depictions of his last days. He loomed over me, offering a heaven, reminding me of a sacrifice I couldn't fathom. And he also watched, with an outstretched arm that might come crashing down in anger or disappointment if I had sex before marriage, drank alcohol, or smoked pot. He was Lord of Rules but also kind, and if you followed the rules, you found space in his heart.

This Jesus had little to say of fear. I didn't hear him curse it the way I would hear some evangelicals speak of fear in later years, but maybe he didn't think much about it at all. It was during college when I first recognized Jesus as one who might physically displace my fear.

Eighteen and home for my first fall break, I picked up my then-boyfriend and headed to the mall for new clothes. All the Black UVA girls seemed to have better style—less frumpy tees and corduroy, more tight-fitting pants and shirts. "Wait, Ohio has more than cows?" my friends liked to joke.

I followed the car in front of me as I drove around the mall perimeter, searching for the entrance. The car ahead slowed, I slowed. The car stopped, I stopped. The car in front of me turned left, I turned le—

"Shit!" was all I heard. The crash a silent whirl.

My navy-blue Volvo with the rebuilt engine turned 180 degrees in the opposite direction, no time to watch the world spin around me. A gold sedan hobbled over to a parking spot, its hood crumpled.

*I'm going to die. This is it.*

"Are you alright?" he asked.

"No!" I must be bleeding internally. My face burned, layers of skin peeled like a potato off my chin from the air bag.

Inside the ambulance, I lay on a stretcher, oxygen tunneling through my nostrils, my heart rate above two hundred. "God, if you save me," I prayed in my head, "I'll do whatever you want." A true Hail Mary, not the one I'd learned in Sunday school. I saw no burning bush, no vision of Jesus healing my back as my mom once described seeing, while she writhed in pain in a hospital bed. But after I'd been bandaged and cleared to go home with minor injuries, I felt a need I couldn't explain. I wanted a Bible.

"Sure, babe," Dad said on our way back to Charlottesville. He called all of us girls "babe," a funny mismatch for how loud and sharp his voice could sound in conversation. He could go from tenor to soprano whether we were discussing Arby's latest sandwich or voter suppression. "We can stop at that Barnes and Noble on the way, and if they don't have one you like, I can get one for you." Brick-and-mortar Christian bookstores were still a thing back then, and wouldn't you know Darryl could find the Bible in any translation you wanted, in burgundy or black faux leather, and all at a discounted price.

I chose a paperback Bible with waxy, thin pages. New Living Translation would allow me to read without stumbling over *thou* and *thee*. I sat atop my bed's purple comforter after Dad left and turned to Genesis. No one told me that the Old Testament could be a tricky place to start. Every time the earth swallowed people whole or someone was judged for what seemed like a small offense, I shut the Bible. Couldn't do it. I'd grab my books for class and wait outside for the bus or trolley, and, without a doubt, every time, I felt a strange disruption in my body. The absence of peace. A chaotic loneliness. I opened that thick book again the next day without making any promises. I missed what I couldn't understand.

If God has a million ways to reach people, he used the I-can't-explain-this-feeling tactic on me. I don't have a great explanation for why I started to fill myself with words I could barely pronounce, with scenes that terrified me, with a God who at times seemed too angry to befriend, let alone follow. Maybe it's the way I can't tell you, without looking, what colors the walls are in my house, but I can tell you how I feel in a particular room. Even how I often don't remember the exact details of a memory but rather its shape. Maybe a God who wanted to reach me would have no choice but to cut through the dread I carried in my chest.

I did not grab a megaphone and yell Bible verses at my fellow classmates or get a tattoo of my favorite scripture, but I did start hanging out with a group of Black Christians on Grounds who sang and held cookouts and listened to preachers on Friday nights. I did start staying up until two and three in the morning journaling about this Jesus, about the voice I heard in the quiet, about the mystery of loving someone I couldn't see, let alone comprehend. Wondering if grace could be real, if fear would persist. Wondering if God had answered my prayer in the ambulance by drawing me closer to words.

Through much of college, I experienced God in the absence of fear. He offered life on the other side of anxiety. I even traveled to South Africa one summer, an eighteen-hour flight one way, to volunteer with campus ministers. If I could spend five weeks halfway around the world without panic, perhaps God had completely removed my fear—exchanged the weight of the irrational for a much lighter sense of possibility.

I tried again and again to fit Tophs's illness into this framework for God. God would be found in the lifting of a burden, not so much the sharing of it. He'd be found on the other side of tears, not so much in the weeping itself. And if divine relief didn't come soon enough, maybe I could help us find it.

Several days after Paul and I heard the term *outlier*, after the sludge had thinned and my limbs felt like mine again, I pulled up behind the desk and tried my luck once more. I didn't think anything could haunt me as much as the title of Malcolm Gladwell's book already had anyway. Tophs was still meeting with Liz and Anita every week, spinning circles in a swing before learning new vocabulary words, and this—moving my fingers along the internet's landscape—felt good. Like action, control even. And illicit, like something I should hide, especially from God, even Paul. People of faith didn't turn to empty search boxes. They turned to the Bible and prayer.

But I kept telling myself I had the right to do this. I had tried waiting. Maybe I could use my internet detective skills to give God a nudge in the right direction. *We're still here.* I overrode the gut check, pressed on.

*hypoglycemia short stature developmental delay*

Maybe I added *carnitine deficiency* or traded *short stature* with *failure to thrive* in one search. What I found, though, seemed like home. Russell-Silver syndrome. I read from the NIH website again: *Babies with this condition have low birth weight and often fail to grow and gain weight at the expected rate (failure to thrive). Head growth is normal, however, so the head may appear unusually large compared to the rest of the body. Affected children are thin and have poor appetites, and some develop recurrent episodes of low blood sugar (hypoglycemia) as a result of feeding difficulties.*

The pictures of children I found online didn't remind me of Tophs, but I read over and over that the phenotype of children with RSS varied greatly. This could be it. I wish I could say humility flooded me when I came across this diagnosis, especially because Dr. Quillian had politely but quickly shut down my concern about Smith-Magenis syndrome. But really it was more like: *Oh my god! Which stay-at-home mom with a humanities degree solved this case? You're lookin' at her!*

I texted my sister Sienna. *Doesn't this sound like Tophs?* I asked. She wrote back, *Hmm, kinda.* But then she sent a link to a study about a kid with a glycogen storage disease. She thought that description fit him better. I read it as I walked by the greeting card aisles in Target and couldn't disagree. The hypoglycemia that led to an ER visit, the developmental delay, the poor growth. But wouldn't they have caught that on Tophs's chromosomal microarray? Wouldn't *someone* have caught it?

I could not be stopped. I joined a Facebook group and followed threads from parents of children with RSS. Everyone commenting understood what it was like to buy size twelve-to-eighteen-month clothing for a three-year-old. They recommended buying wetsuits for the pool or beach because, like Tophs, their kids couldn't adjust to cold water. These moms, too, had worried about their child's glucose level dropping overnight.

Our family could live with this.

We would go to the national conference in Chicago, stay with my sister Autumn's family, and learn everything there was to know about RSS. A genetic test could confirm the diagnosis. Tophs would take growth hormones, do a few extra push-ups in middle school, and go to the prom one day.

13

New genetic tests could sever the rope from around my waist. If the doctors found mutations in Tophs's genes, we'd be forced to look back to conception, preconception, even God, who is way bigger than any mistake I might have made as a mother. If these problems had been there *in the beginning*, then I'd be free to respond to, rather than atone for. God himself, the maker of bodies, would be the "ram in the bush," or scapegoat, and my sense of self would survive. Even if my hope for a diagnosis had been battered, our search didn't feel complete. No one had sent us home or told us we were out of options.

The next wave of tests started with Shelley. Tall, with an Elsa braid that hung over her shoulder, Shelley greeted us and sat down at the computer. Her eyes were Disney blue and direct, but not unkind. I resisted her role at first. She was young and engaging, but she wasn't the geneticist. And the only thing worse than not knowing how to tell your son's story—to relay the scope of puzzling issues without getting lost in details—is muddling through that story twice in one day.

It turned out Shelley wasn't a resident or medical school student; she was a genetic counselor, guiding families by way of Punnett squares and lab orders, through what genetics had to offer them.

"Is there any chance you two are related?" she asked us.

"Uhhh, we don't think so?" Paul and I laughed, but I quietly added another possible failure to my list: failure to marry someone outside my own family tree. I'd been so careful about making sure Paul was the right person for me.

Before we got engaged, Paul and I fasted forty days, Moses style; we progressively ate less and less until we were sipping ramen noodles at dusk, delirious with salt and zeal. We would either hear God clearly or die of hypertension. On the last day of the fast, Paul drove down to Charlottesville and knocked on the door of my Lawn room, a wooden closet without a bathroom that was supposedly an honor to live inside. Fasting guides suggest eating light or bland foods when you first break a fast, so Paul naturally brought Five Guys in two brown sacks, the bottoms translucent with grease. We sat down at my makeshift dining table, and I hadn't even finished my burger when he said we should take a walk to the Rotunda.

"I'm not done!" I protested, grabbing a handful of Cajun-style fries. I don't remember putting shoes on, but I do remember climbing onto his back as we crossed the Lawn to the bottom of the stairs. A guy sitting off to the left got up and walked away, and I looked to see rose petals sprinkled on each step. At the top, a vase of seven roses, one for each month we'd officially, officially dated, and then this fine man had the nerve to turn toward me, open his mouth, and sing "Ribbon in the Sky." He pulled me in and we danced as he transitioned from Stevie to side B of my birth tape, where I sang the alphabet. "Tell me what you think of me," he whisper-sang in my ear. "I think you're wonderful, Taylor."

He knelt. "Yes," I said, but he didn't hear it over my giggles; I am terribly awkward in real life. "*Yes*! I said yes!" I also hate repeating myself, but the dude had a brand-new ring. Paul had spent the last year eating bread and mac 'n' cheese in order to save enough money. We went back to my room, where I promptly finished my food before we called our families. I woke throughout the night, forgetting and remembering and remembering again that the princess-cut diamond on the thin band was mine.

Paul had driven to Ohio and stayed in my grandmother's spare bedroom to ask my parents for their blessing at a coffee shop. I don't blame them for being terrified; I'd be the first and youngest to get married. I studied something called humanities. They gave a hesitant yes with contingency clauses. But at least it wasn't a no.

This appointment wasn't the right time to tell Shelley about the Moses fast and Five Guys, but it strikes me now that the question she really asked us was: *Are the odds already stacked against your child?*

"I'm sorry," she said. "We have to ask everyone that."

Beneath that question lurked another I'd already started to ask myself: What were my expectations—of my child and his body, of myself and my body? Had I expected near perfection or ease? And what about the man I'd fallen for and so carefully prayed about marrying—did I expect him to be free of misspelled genes?

My expectations didn't matter to the lab where Shelley would send Tophs's blood. It could have been the precision of Shelley's outfit—a sleeveless blouse and pencil skirt—or the clarity and quickness of the words coming from her straight, white teeth, but in that moment, I found comfort in what I perceived to be the hard lines of genetics. The department, housed on the fifth floor of the children's hospital, might as well have been an exclusive VIP club to me. These doctors could pinpoint with scary precision where a gene took a left turn, where it picked up an extra letter or left one out, and what that change meant. While we'd seen the chief before, we had more information about Tophs's development this time, as well as a strong referral from Dr. Perry. Tophs either had a genetic disease or he didn't. We'd just have to wait to find out.

Shelley methodically led us through a list of questions. Paul and I each answered for our own sides of the family because, together, we had made this person. We believed God had created him but knew our boy wasn't exactly made from dust.

*Does anyone in your family have thyroid issues? Learning disabilities? Autoimmune disease? Anemia?*

I cycled through every person I knew in my family, every story I'd inherited. Most answers were an easy no, but Paul and I were careful to consider a cousin or niece on one side or the other who might have struggled in school or been hospitalized with persistent fevers. Shelley had tossed us a net, and our job was to place any debris, no matter how old or ragged, into that net and allow her and the geneticist to sort through the pieces. *My mom might have a clotting issue* and *I think she's allergic to iodine* and *She's sensitive to anesthesia* got thrown in alongside the definitive answers: *There's no history of glaucoma* and *No, I don't smoke.* Shelley took notes, and while she didn't write down every memory or half story I shared, she didn't let on that a particular detail was irrelevant.

Once when Eliot was sick, I'd kept a careful hand-drawn calendar with notes about her illness for the doctor. When I handed the paper to the visiting pediatrician, she took one look at it, held it far from her face, as though it was trash, and handed it right back. I couldn't know if she dismissed me because of my race or my youth, or because I was a stay-at-home mom, or because she was just arrogant.

Dismissal was not the vibe I got from Shelley. "Okay, I'm going to share this information with Dr. Humberson, and then we'll be back in."

I had no idea who Dr. Humberson was. That was the nature of referrals. I showed up, hoping a stranger held the answer that had previously eluded another stranger. Within minutes, Dr. Humberson, lean, with an athletic build, joined us. She wore a white coat over slacks and flats, her brown hair pulled back at the top. She shared the same steadiness and confidence I sensed from Shelley, as well as genuine concern. She was, I learned, a mom.

I watched her feel Tophs's head, measure his wingspan, touch his toes. I pretended not to know the mental list of phenotypic characteristics she was checking off. His small triangular chin. The size of his head in relation to the rest of his body. Did his forehead protrude more than my own?

Dr. Humberson finished and turned to us. "We should test him for fragile X syndrome, but I don't think he has it. We check every boy his age with developmental delays." Then she said the sweetest words I'd ever heard. "He has some features that are consistent with something called Russell-Silver syndrome."

I hadn't even mentioned my own research. What could be more validating? I was basically a lay geneticist.

"Now the test for Russell-Silver isn't perfect. It only picks up 35 to 50 percent of cases, so even if the test comes back normal, we can't necessarily rule it out." *Okay, maybe genetics wasn't all black-and-white.* She continued. "In some cases, a clinical diagnosis can be made, but I'm not sure that's a fit for Christopher."

His perfect cheekbones, the large head he might grow into, the short and scrawny legs he used to jump off tables. The deep, wide eyes that invited you in. His moderately low but not unheard-of birthweight. The button nose without a bridge he shared with Eliot. I couldn't disagree with Dr. Humberson. Without a positive test result, Tophs wouldn't be a slam dunk for RSS.

"If neither test comes back positive, I agree with Dr. Perry that it's reasonable to consider whole exome sequencing."

*Every new wave of genetic testing.*

I know Dr. Humberson explained the test to us; her notes say so. *I discussed with the patient's parents that whole exome sequencing is a relatively newly available clinical blood test that sequences the protein-coding regions of about 20,000 of our genes simultaneously.* But I don't remember that conversation.

What rises to the surface is Paul, ever so carefully, tossing a glass bottle, the note tucked deep inside, to Dr. Humberson. He is a boy and a father, a protector and a beggar, all at once.

"I know it's hard to predict, but what do you think? How do you think he'll do?"

She catches it. Holds it. Turns the bottle over, unwraps the origami, the flesh of a father's heart. "I think his social skills will get him far," she says, her eyes steady, holding our faces. Her words are not the great ship come to save us; they could be light in the darkness. Could be the widow's mite, a doctor's humble but meaningful gift.

Dr. Humberson left, and so did Paul and the kids, though I'm not certain where he took them. I only know I sat in that spare white room with a pamphlet in my hands and Shelley's voice in my ear. Even if my memory isn't whole, it's accurate: When I first met whole exome sequencing, I was alone with Shelley. Since then, I've kept her near.

I looked down at the graphic of a double helix, a roller coaster of cells, and remembered my AP Biology teacher who fed us fresh popcorn on special movie days. *Twenty thousand genes. Results in three to four months. I'll work on getting preauthorization. We'll also need samples from you and Paul.*

As long as it wouldn't hurt Tophs or cost too much, we'd rather over-test him. Tophs still barely squirmed when a needle broke his skin. It was one of the ways we knew, along with watching him fall and bang his head without crying, that he was underresponsive to pain. He'd get up, touch his hand to his head, and keep moving.

The pamphlet included drawings of chromosomes as turquoise Xs and listed possible test results, including the good (benign), the bad (pathogenic), and the place we'd been landing for the past year (unknown). There was a chance, Shelley explained, that even if the lab found a mutation, or variant, in one of Tophs's genes, we still might not know the significance of that change. If everyone in the world underwent whole exome sequencing, we'd find a lot of mutations—some benign, some never before seen, as well as those known to be more dangerous. And even the "dangerous" mutations didn't necessarily guarantee that disease had already invaded or would one day invade a person's body. Each of our family trees likely hold notches in the wood that make our particular tribe distinct, give us character. Sometimes nothing more, nothing less.

But were we getting ahead of ourselves? We still didn't have the answer to the Russell-Silver test. If that came back positive, we might not even need whole exome sequencing. RSS seemed big enough to capture Tophs's slow growth, hypoglycemia, and developmental delays. Those three were often listed as his main medical concerns.

I appreciated Shelley and Dr. Humberson's solid plan. I could tell they were brilliant, knew the ropes. So I listened intently, trying to capture the basic outline of this test that might help us know the innermost parts of our son. We came to the geneticist's office because doctors referred us. We came because this appointment, like the others, was typed into our family Google calendar with an alert. But we came with a primal need: we were two parents looking for the very boy we'd brought with us.

I knew that rhythm and counting made sense to Tophs when other things did not. I knew that I should not read the words inside Mo Willems's white speech boxes if I didn't want him to throw the book. But I could use that book as a makeshift pillow for his head as I tickled him just to hear his deep belly laugh, see his eyes anticipate my fingers, and know without a doubt he was mine. Still, there was a day-to-day feeling, more of a dull, persistent ache, hard to fit into words. My chief concern as Tophs's mother remained this sense that I couldn't consistently get through to him—as though he were a place, and I was an eager but frustrated traveler who might never reach it.

"You have the option with whole exome sequencing to test

what we call *actionable* genes," Shelley informed me. "This is a group of over fifty genes, where if we find a mutation, we can take action to prevent the disease associated with the mutation. For example, we wouldn't test for a mutation associated with Alzheimer's, because we can't take any steps to prevent it. But we can test for mutations associated with certain cancers and diseases that we're able to screen for ahead of time."

Even though she said the lab wouldn't screen for Alzheimer's, it lodged in my mind as the prime example of what could come back with these results. There was a chance I'd learn new information about my son (or his future) that would terrify me. I could walk around with a new burden unrelated to the reasons we'd come to see Dr. Humberson. But that possible burden lived too far out there, too distant from the present, for me to feel its weight. In the Church, we speak of scripture dropping from our heads to our hearts as the ultimate goal. But in this circumstance, giving myself time to process the risk of scary results seemed irrational.

I signed the form to test those fifty-plus genes. I wanted to turn to Paul and ask, *Is this fishing? Do we want to know, no matter the cost?* Those were the questions that played on a reel through my mind as I walked out of the hospital, past kids in wheelchairs and adults leaving outpatient surgery. But when I checked in with Paul later at home, he agreed. "I think we'd want to know, especially if we could do something about it."

A few days after my twenty-seventh birthday, when the first two pink lines emerged on a pregnancy test, I walked upstairs and found Paul, and we knelt by the bed. We were grateful and also eager to pray for the baby's health. That no illness would transfer from us to the fetus. Even though Paul had experienced depression early in our marriage during his PhD program, I didn't yet see it as an underlying or chronic condition. More like a one-time occurrence tied to stressful circumstances. *Temporary.* When we prayed about certain illnesses stopping with *us*, we were praying about my anxiety, that it would be cut off with the umbilical cord. At that time, I believed identifying which addictions or disorders lived on which branches of the family tree, coupled with God's help, would protect my children. We knew it would take God's hand because we'd seen what happened when I tried to do it on my own.

The apostle Paul asked God to release him. To take the thorn from his flesh. He wrote, "Concerning this thing I pleaded with the Lord three times that it might depart from me." God, unworried, responded, "My grace is sufficient for you, for My strength is made perfect in weakness."

My last year of college, when I was in love with my Paul and Jesus, feeling all-powerful and zealous, I tried to unthorn myself. I informed God that his grace was so sufficient, I could wean myself off Paxil. I started to taper off the medicine I'd taken religiously since high school. Like a proud Peter, I would, pill by half pill, step out of the restrictive boat of Medicine and walk on water. Though I never asked Jesus if he was calling me to these waves. Of course, God wanted me to have faith. What could be more godly?

Over three months, without a word to my mother or Dr. Dawdy, because I didn't want anyone changing my mind, I decreased from fifteen milligrams to nothing. For the first couple of months, I felt great. Untethered, impressed by my complete reliance on God. Then came a few brain zaps here, an irrational fear there. But I was engaged, in love. Next, my mind raced with obsessive thoughts: What did it mean to blaspheme the Holy Spirit, and had I done it? By winter's end, I sat on the ledge of my mother's bathtub in Columbus and reasoned it'd be best for me to die and see Jesus, to make sure he'd welcome me home. I didn't want to be left behind.

In the cool of my mother's basement, I called Paul, crying, told him I couldn't do it anymore. I was scared and tired. So scared all the time.

"Tell God, sweetheart," his voice an anchor to the living world. "Jesus, please help her, Jesus," he prayed.

The Paxil took weeks to kick back in, and I had to promise Dr. Dawdy I would never again quit on my own. Mom drove me back to school for my last semester and slept on my floor for a few nights as I reoriented to normal life. I wondered if Paul would call off the wedding. It was one thing to love a woman who had an anxiety disorder. It was quite another to spend forever with a woman who'd had a complete breakdown.

He stayed, and his father married us that summer on a large wooden deck overlooking a gray-brown river in Ohio. Five years later, Eliot's gray-green eyes opened before us. I got lost watching her sleep: one cheek pressed against the crib mattress, her chest holding and releasing, holding and releasing her breaths, and I thought, I could do this again. Before I'd stopped nursing, before my cycle returned, nausea crept in, and I couldn't even find a probable date on the calendar. As the nurse practitioner held her wand and looked at the screen, she asked, "How did you even know you were pregnant? You're only about four weeks."

As though this child, the second, came out of nowhere. After we brought him home from the hospital, he shed like a snake, his new skin a deep red-brown. He looked like neither of us, maybe my grandmother or father. He smiled so soon and had just enough silky brown hair for a baby mohawk. Tophs did not resemble his sister, except for the same elfish nose, perfectly proportioned lips, and those curly eyelashes that got us all here in the first place. And as he grew, the two shared the same deep belly giggle. You can tell a Harris kid a million miles away by their laugh. But who was *this* Harris?

I'm not sure Paul has ever needed to answer that question, at least not in the same way. I've always known how much he cares about Tophs. How much he trusts God. And we've learned together that we can't just fix everything on our own, that even if we pray the "right" prayer, God doesn't necessarily give us what we want. Maybe *doing something* is a mix of science and faith, of hard work and prayer, of searching and disappointment.

Days after our genetics appointment with Shelley, as we waited for insurance to authorize the tests, I sent him a one-liner email with a link:

*I know you think I'm Crazy Balls, but if we had a diagnosis I would go to this in Chicago.*

*This* was an annual convention for families of children who had Russell-Silver syndrome or had been Small for Gestational Age (SGA). My idea of a plan.

He responded: *If nothing else, communicating with other parents through this medium could probably be helpful too. Thanks for sharing.*

Thanks for sharing. Have a nice day. Who was this guy?

I nudged him again one Sunday morning during church. With Tophs and Eliot well cared for in the kids' ministry and my husband's arm next to mine, my thoughts turned to Tophs. "Do you think he has it?" I leaned over, whispering. I was a child, seeking permission to wonder.

"I think he might." I felt a rush of validation before the sadness. "Some of the characteristics fit. He'll definitely need intervention."

I've learned that even though Paul is a counselor who listens well and loves talking to people, he doesn't readily offer his feelings about Tophs's health. A person can be really good at posing questions to others, can be honest and live with nothing to hide, and still need a reminder to let themselves feel. I need action-oriented Paul on my team to pull me out of the dregs. There are days, still, when I can barely move from under the weight of this search, but that's not what parenting Tophs has looked like on Paul's body. It's only now I understand he needs me—to stuff his plans in a drawer some days and say, "I'm sad. How about you?"

Maybe Paul didn't spend hours ruminating on Tophs's development, but he'd noticed. Like in the text message he'd sent when I'd grown frustrated trying to engage Tophs at home. I wasn't alone. Somewhere between teaching classes and preparing sermons for seminary and local churches, between making beats for the kids as they danced and cooking them waffles, Paul was thinking, maybe even *feeling*, something about what life might look like for Tophs.

In our marriage, I need Paul to remind me that the tomb is empty, that Christ is risen, that he will set all things right one day. But Paul needs me to remind him that for three long days, the whole world groaned in darkness and betrayal, that sometimes our lives feel too much like the evening of day two.

## 14

Is it horrible to want your child to have *something*?

Shelley called. The first round of tests were normal. Tophs did not have fragile X syndrome, no surprise there. But he didn't test positive for Russell-Silver syndrome, either. I hadn't cracked the code. Once again, I tiptoed along an uncomfortable but familiar high wire, thanking God for what my son didn't have and wondering if we'd ever find out what he did. Russell-Silver had seemed like a manageable syndrome that would have connected me with doctors who understood my son, or at least some of his traits and challenges. A negative meant no penciled-in trajectory, no "We've been there, and here's what you might see."

I grieved the loss of my would-be friends, whom I'd already talked to on Facebook about growth hormone shots and wetsuits for kids with no body fat. I grieved the hope of belonging. I'd felt this back in high school, as I realized I could never be an upper-middle-class white girl. But now I mourned community for my son and for us as his parents. I thanked Shelley and told her we'd get our blood drawn so that our samples could join Tophs's in the lab that would sort through his exome, maybe the way dry cleaners sort through the mechanical rack of blazers and dresses until your garment is found.

This test would be our last stop. The best-case scenario? By sending off Tophs's DNA, we'd be able to map him out, discover what made him slow to respond to pain or his name. Or know why he could eat ice cream and pizza before bed and still have dangerously low glucose levels by morning. It was August, so with analysis taking about four months, I could expect results before Christmas.

We also moved that summer, from the place of student-run gardens, dining halls, and picnic-table jumping to a beige Cape Cod in the city of Charlottesville. All because I'd met with a campus minister who mentioned his old house was for sale. I fell in love with the stars laid into the fireplace hearth and dormers that let great light into the kids' bedroom. Paul loved the basement apartment we could rent out to pay the mortgage. The neighborhood was even zoned for the elementary school where Paige taught a special education preschool class. The city would test Tophs, and if he was found eligible, there was a chance Paige would be his teacher. It all seemed too big to be a coincidence. We hadn't even been looking for a house.

Tophs certainly wasn't worried about any test results that summer, which could have been the grace of youth, or a grace of Tophs. We continued his weekly speech and OT appointments, where he learned to touch shaving cream and visited a special kitchen to try new foods. As he sat at a long table, Anita presented him with small, hard breadsticks and a can of spray cheese. I tried to "fix my face," as my friends would say, when Anita squirted the orange whipped cream onto a plate. I love food, but I'm picky; Lunchables terrified me, even as kid. Cold sauce on a cracker does not a pizza make. But Tophs took a stick, dipped it into the cheese, and tasted it. His smooth brown face broke into delight. "Mmmm, delicious!" he said. *He said delicious!* I would buy a hundred cans of processed cheese to hear him say those words. Really, there was no key to understanding which words Tophs picked up and why. One of his favorites to use in imaginative play was *conference*. Paul would fly to academic conferences for work and send videos to the kids from his hotel room between sessions. So Tophs's figurines flew to conferences too.

Yet, even as Anita and Liz noted his progress, how he connected more words with meanings, they still emphasized placing him in a full-day public preschool. "Christopher has had a language explosion," Anita wrote. But we weren't in the clear. He couldn't yet answer, What is your name? How old are you? Are you a boy or a girl? *Tophs . . . three . . . boy.* We couldn't make those responses, ghosts as they were, come from his lips.

In the fall, as we began the eligibility process with the city schools, Paige invited Tophs to a speech circle in her classroom on the mornings he didn't have preschool at the church. Her room was as open and delightful as she was. We walked in one day to see Tophs's picture and name on the back of a plastic chair. Tophs had a place. They had made room for him, even though he was only a visitor. When the group moved to a table for a lesson involving food and Tophs struggled to reach ingredients, Paige asked the custodian about lowering the table. A boy with bright blond hair sat with a weighted blanket on his legs at circle time. Another boy, with warm, brown curls, breathed through a ventilator and had his own tabletop attached to his wheelchair. His nurse touched sweet ingredients from cooking projects to his lips. One student, who seemed small in stature like Tophs but had the vocabulary of a first or second grader, sat in a wheelchair, sometimes moving his finger along a tablet to sort insects as he waited for other students to arrive. He had a wry way about him, wore pink socks, and adored My Little Pony, just as Tophs would come to. His name was Bennett. And I remember longing after his mind for my son, hoping his clarity of speech and thought might rub off on Tophs. Bennett, the peer model. Bennett, the Brony, as they call boys who love My Little Pony. One day Paige told me that Tophs and Bennett moved down the halls of the elementary school together, Tophs holding on to his friend's chair. That image—the two of them moving through the world together—felt sacred. No longer did special education seem like the cordoned-off space for "others" I'd perceived as a kid.

We received copies of Tophs's academic results ahead of his first preschool eligibility meeting. Packets made of white paper, blocks of dark text, rectangular tables with numbers. This was my son's educational DNA, as best we could track it. When I read the words in those boxes, I had to swallow, and my eyes burned as though I'd applied liquid soap for mascara. *Delayed, low average, fifth percentile.*

*We need the help, we want the help—this hurts like hell.*

One assessor noted, "His inability to process and respond to questions is the most problematic at this time." *I wish I had no idea what she was talking about*. Our son's cognitive ability, she wrote, was hard to determine because of his speech delay. We shouldn't take every low score to heart, because it was hard to get a good read on kids so young. But we also couldn't assume that once his language improved, everything else would fall into place.

Under one table of standard scores and percentiles, Paul had written *Language—impacting other areas of learning*. And next to that, *chicken or egg?* Paul and I tend to read these reports separately, make notes in the margins, and then talk after the kids go to bed. We've read several reports about Tophs over the years, and I still have to push myself to admit to Paul how heavy these numbers and words feel in my body.

The eligibility meeting only lasted a full hour because we had to review the results as a group. Paul and I didn't have to prove anything. The educators around the table who'd spent time with Tophs knew he qualified. And by God's grace, they placed Tophs in Paige's special education classroom. We couldn't have written that plan ourselves.

Still, after reading those test results and talking to the educators, I returned home, wanting to Google "What do I do with this pain?" I am drawn to pain, I confess. I don't go searching for it, but if our paths cross, if it latches onto me as I'm walking, I will wrest its legs from around my waist, peel its head off my chest, hold it far away, my elbows locked, my arms straightened, and then pull it back close to my face. I want to know everything about this pain, even if it hurts.

In a picture Paige sent from Tophs's first week in her class, he's sitting next to a friend at the table. The students have constructed Thanksgiving turkeys with crackers, Nutter Butters, candy corn, and peanut butter chips. Tophs's face is turned toward his friend, cracked wide with joy, his eyes scrunched up by his full cheeks, his mouth wide with a grin. There is a place for him. The photo, true and beautiful and good, also served as a marker. We were sliding farther away from What Was.

Tophs wears dark-rinse jeans rolled up at the bottom, a striped tee, and tiny soft-soled Pumas in a photo from Before. He holds Paul's hand as they stand on the pavement outside the dorm. His hair, a fuzzy mix of curls and strays, halos his head. It's sunny, and Paul's slacks cast a shadow that runs parallel to the one created by Tophs's body. At sixteen months, he is one month away from walking. He's smaller but still following the path of his older sister, who walked at seventeen months. And, aside from slow weight gain, nothing atypical has caught and held our attention. We are free to stand in the heat and consider dinner or teething or college savings plans.

A friend of mine, whose daughter contracted bacterial meningitis as a toddler, sometimes wonders who her daughter, who survived the illness but lost her hearing and had to relearn so much, might have been if the illness never found her. There is, flitting in and out of her thoughts, a ghost of her girl, and she doesn't need anyone to tell her to love the daughter here in front of her. She needs someone to keep vigil as she mourns the girl she knew and lost. She needs someone to sit round the fire with her and burn or bury or whittle new expectations from branches that had grown in the soils of life Before.

# 15

What a waste," I said to myself, setting the pregnancy test on the back of the toilet. We'd just returned from our annual Thanksgiving trip to Ohio, and I'd picked up a test at Target on a silly hunch, a thin chance of *what if*?

I hadn't told Paul that a little part of me wasn't ready to call it quits.

"Our plate is full," he'd said. "To me, our family feels complete." On the outside, I nodded. Another kid could do me in. I could barely locate my nipples, let alone remember how to nurse a newborn. All the while, in a mental picture I couldn't quite explain, a rounding out of our family was missing. Wrapped in my silence about a possible third child was the greatest difference between Paul and me: capacity. Paul, the Harlem Globetrotter, spinning a ball on one finger, juggling two more with his feet. He worked while he got his PhD in counselor education, he attended seminary while he taught at UVA. Meanwhile, I'm the kid in the corner of the gym, working hard to dribble one ball, hoping I don't get a wedgie. Why in the world would I add more stress? Not to mention the depressing nausea that lasted nine months.

But a small window of opportunity had opened that wasn't all my fault. Earlier that month, the OB/GYN's office had called in the wrong strength of birth control on a Friday night, and when Paul bought backup contraception from the corner store, I told him I hadn't waited twenty-two years to have sex for his ratchet gas-station condoms. We would take our chances. His vasectomy was only a month away anyhow.

I looked one more time at the plastic stick I'd set down. There, a new second line on the test window, the faintest line I'd ever seen, as though it had to gather courage to cross the white space. It was impossible, but I had already known.

I texted Paul at work: *Um I think I might be pregnant.*
*You think???*

I worried Paul might be mad, and I worried that I didn't have the energy for another child. If the past few years were any indication, Paul would probably never work just one nine-to-five. Still, I floated nine thousand miles above ground because this baby had squeezed through some tight hoops to get here. Later, my friend Remington would drag me for texting my husband the news. Obviously, she'd never heard of a *scheduled* vasectomy.

Focus, I told myself. Eliot would turn five the next day, and she deserved all the attention in the world; we'd already given so much to Tophs. I would reflect on going into slow, painful labor five years before and Paul driving me to a Home Depot for his distraction-by-way-of-plywood strategy. I'd buy ice cream sandwiches for Eliot's preschool celebration and deliver them at snack time.

When a 434 number popped up on my phone that afternoon, I left Eliot in a full prebirthday tantrum on the living room floor next to our Christmas tree and walked into the kitchen. Before I even heard a voice, my pulse quickened.

"We have the results of Tophs's genetic testing," Shelley said. "Is this a good time?"

I don't know. *Is* this a good time? "Only one kid's screaming, so it's great," I joked. Stolen levity. I grabbed a piece of paper and pen. If anyone was going to get to the bottom of this, I knew it would be Shelley.

"So there are three results I want to talk to you about."

The world is on fire and I cannot see it. I wrote to not miss anything. I wrote because what else would I do?

Once again, only Shelley and I existed in a white-walled portal. Shelley, there on behalf of science. Me, on behalf of my son. The first mutation was found in a gene that causes an autosomal recessive disorder. Autosomal means the gene isn't sex specific, and recessive means Tophs would need two changes to develop the actual disorder, in this case glycogen storage disease. Had Sienna been onto something with her text? But he only had one change, so he didn't have the disease. "Not found in me or Paul," I scribbled in parentheses. No blame here. We didn't cause this quirk. *De novo*, they call it, literally meaning "of new."

According to what Shelley and science knew at this point, Tophs's single mutation did not matter clinically. He was a carrier and should consider his status before having kids, but his particular misspelling wasn't known to cause symptoms. One down.

Shelley described the second finding: the lab detected two mutations in a gene that is known to cause a recessive disorder related to bone size. One mutation came from Paul, one from me. "We haven't seen this particular misspelling before," she explained. "It could be a benign familial change." She used the words *variant of unknown significance*, and I wished I had paid better attention to that pamphlet she'd given me. A VUS means there's a change in a genetic sequence, but science hasn't yet determined whether that change is potentially harmful or benign. It could carry a risk of disease, or not. Tophs's short stature could be related to this mutation, or not. Genetics has this way of being completely specific—pinpointing the exact erroneous sequence within the exact gene—and still not locating you in time and space and significance.

Shelley's voice signaled she was winding down. We would not solve this case today. She paused, and I assumed I'd misunderstood her, there were only two results. Or maybe the two mutations, one from Paul and one from me, counted as separate results. "The last result is actually a secondary finding," she said. "Do you remember how you and Paul agreed to have us look at those actionable genes?"

Actionable genes. Like cancer genes. Things you might have time to prevent. A chance to cheat death.

"Wait, who is this about?"

"Yeah, I know this is a bit scary." Shelley's voice is a tonal apology. "Have you heard of the BRCA mutation? We found that your son has this mutation, and so do you."

I am fourteen again on that flight to Spain for spring break. Only this time, there's no fear that my throat will close up mid-flight; this time, the fear is that cancer cells are already hidden in my breasts or ovaries, waiting to multiply. And no one can guarantee my new thought is irrational.

*What is it called when we have every right to fear?*

I knew exactly what BRCA was. Lindsay, my friend who sat next to me on that flight, whose mother survived breast and ovarian cancer, had both breasts removed in her twenties because of it. As Shelley talked, I envisioned the cemetery up Route 29, across from the Target Tophs loved so much. Is that where I would be laid to rest?

"The BRCA2 mutation is associated with an increased risk of breast and ovarian cancer." And as though she'd read my mind, "This doesn't mean you have or will get cancer."

She emphasized the risk as *adult onset* and said care looks different for men than women. What did this mean for my son, who had no breasts or ovaries, who still peed in a pull-up and watched *Daniel Tiger*? Daniel visited the doctor for X-rays or shots, not to discuss his predisposition to certain kinds of cancer. "This won't change Tophs's care now, but he will need certain screenings in the future."

And what about my birthday girl?

"She has a 50 percent chance of having the mutation. And so do your siblings . . . One of your parents must carry it . . ."

"Shelley," my voice the wing of a dragonfly, "I guess I should tell you now. I took a pregnancy test this morning, and it was positive." Had I just confessed or asked for help? Either way, I hid within my throat, calling out to Shelley and science and God that I hadn't been given the chance to *not* conceive a baby. It was too late. This seed, this baby, I just *knew* she was a girl. She had no breasts yet, and I was already threatening to take them away. How do you excise ovaries that don't exist?

"This is so much to process in one day," Shelley said.

I told her I didn't want to hear the numbers yet. Turns out, when it's about my health, I want less information. I don't want to Google. I agreed to take a day before coming to see her.

"I know this is hard to imagine," she said, "but remember, this mutation isn't new. You've always had it. You were born with it. We're just finding out about it now."

I hung up. Everything in my life had prepared me for something other than this. The flight to Spain, the flight from New York, the car crash over fall break. Even Eliot's pneumonia and Tophs's major tests for fragile X or missing chromosomes. Every circumstance had eventually come with a release valve or a divine vote of confidence. But no degree of cognitive behavioral therapy in the world seemed sufficient to hold this. I couldn't protect myself, couldn't protect my children, couldn't promise them Mommy wouldn't get sick. Every single bit of my fear was deserved. A terrifying and lonely place, this corner of the world, this corner of the mind, where you can't rationally talk yourself out of darkness.

When Paul walked in the house from work minutes later, I did the thing I'd wanted to do a hundred times in over a decade of marriage but had been too scared to do: I collapsed into his chest and cried. Fear had masterfully eroded my pride. If fear has one good quality, one saving grace, this is it. I was sliced open, exposed. And Paul, he could not save me from this, could not make a plan to fix it. But he was the closest thing to an antidote. As he stood in our kitchen, his arms around me, and let me lean into his body, my panic dulled.

Paul called a grad student to watch the kids, and I thanked her, a woman whose face I cannot recall, and slipped out the front door into the night.

Just being in the car, sitting next to Paul, the winter's way of becoming midnight at 6:00 p.m., felt a good match for my soul, helped me keep one foot in the world. When panic roars through my body, the world gains more dimensions than my senses can handle. The trees walk, dragging their heels, animals with silver eyes dart in front of us at every turn, and ceiling lights burst through windows of hospitals and homes as we pass by. I needed— I need—my husband's hand to remind me I'm still part of life here, no matter how frightening that might be.

# 16

The next day, I bought Blue Bunny ice cream sandwiches with vanilla wafers and birthday cake ice cream for Eliot's preschool celebration. She had engaged more in class that year, playing dress-up in fake heels and tiaras, even if she sat alone at her table during the morning movement time.

I wanted to tell anyone who would listen about the strange news I'd received. This thing I couldn't turn back from, that would change everything.

Instead, we sang, and this time, all the attention and voices didn't make her cry. Just months before, in an essay published by *The Toast*, I'd wondered publicly about the ways in which I might have passed on my anxiety to Eliot, even though I had prayed so intently that this particular thorn would not pierce her flesh. I wrote:

> *My sweet daughter—who can read and draw and play basketball at home—often stands or sits in the corner of the classroom and the playground and watches. When one of her teachers comes to get her from our minivan at morning drop-off, she freezes, looks straight ahead, and cannot say a word. Just the moment before, she might have been belly laughing or singing. Then, she's gone. They lift her out—a brown doll with a tutu and tights—and stand her up on the ground.*

Two lines later, I ask what turned out to be the most prescient question ever, the echo before the sound:

> *How do moms who pass down a BRCA gene mutation feel?*

I was thinking of my friend Lindsay's mom. When Lindsay became an adult, she took the test and found out she also carried the BRCA1 mutation.

I'd become Lindsay's mom. Had I written his mutation into existence? Of course not. I was born with it. Shelley said so. Had I somehow known or sensed it? I don't think so. After Lindsay became the youngest person in the country at the time to have a prophylactic double mastectomy, she started the organization Bright Pink, and I watched her interviews. I read the profiles written about her. I even copyedited some of her brochures and materials for Bright Pink. I took the five-minute quiz to see if I might have an increased risk of breast or ovarian cancer. I was proud of Lindsay, of the way she dedicated her life to helping women at risk, but I was not one of those women.

My therapist talks about how hard my brain is working, doing its job to keep me alive. That's how brains are designed to work. Mine is just, you know, *doing the most*. I'd worried about cancer before, because both my breasts have always been dense, making monthly self-exams torture. But whereas obsessing over the way my heart pounded as a teenager eventually led to a diagnosis of mitral valve prolapse, I can't say the same for this mutation. Anxiety about my body hadn't led me to this truth. In that essay, I'd merely imagined the BRCA analogy as a vessel, a way to make sense of our bodies' permeability, a way to make room for a mother's guilt.

Everything had changed. I *was* one of those women. The vessel was, in fact, my body, not some flimsy analogy. I showered, wondering if my breasts were poison.

One grace in finding out your child has a BRCA mutation is there's nothing you can do about it. No preventive actions for children exist because the associated cancers are adult onset. There's no need to perform prostrate screenings on a preschooler, and because there's no medical benefit to knowing, Eliot and the new baby couldn't be tested until they became adults. The good news was, I had nothing but time. The bad news was, I had nothing but time to think about the conversations awaiting us.

How would I introduce the idea to Eliot, prone to worry? What about Tophs, who seemed to process visually? Would he want to read the pamphlet and see the charts again and again? Would I talk to each child individually, and, if so, how would I ensure the older two didn't tell the youngest? Or maybe that'd be better. Perhaps Paul, the counselor, could at least open the conversation. I already knew I'd want to disappear.

There were some clear next steps for me, however. At thirty-two, I was ushered into a high-risk screening program at UVA's hospital. Two weeks after my phone call with Shelley, two weeks since she'd drawn Punnett squares for me in a follow-up appointment, I entered the Emily Couric Clinical Cancer Center.

Some things in this country never change. The first person I saw in the lobby was a middle-aged man in a Confederate motorcycle vest and hat. The red bars, crossed in an *X* against dark leather, made me feel right at home. I'm forever scared I'll have to see some of these folks in heaven, but at least they'll be far away from the Spades table. What if they show up in the same vests, just with feathers poking out?

But once I moved past the entrance and began to see more sick people, I felt like an imposter. I hoped I was.

In the waiting area of the gynecologic oncology office, I picked up a glossy magazine. Inside I saw Eliot, picking apples with Paul, in an ad for the Southern Environmental Law Center. A small treasure, as though God had left a trail to let me know he'd been there.

"So how did you end up here and what have you been told?" a staff member asked. It was the first question that didn't require my address or insurance card. *How did you end up here? What have you been told?* This is theology and story, science and myth. Except this was only intake.

I told her about my son, the thousands of genes, the flaw they'd found that led right back to me. She gave me handouts in a blue folder. There were numbers on those handouts—my lifetime risk of breast cancer could top 80 percent. The lower end was about 46 percent. Even if I were genetically and environmentally located near the lower end, I'd still have about a fifty-fifty chance of getting breast cancer.

Then Dr. Modesitt, the high-risk program's director, an energetic and wiry woman with glasses and wavy hair, performed a manual breast exam. She talked fast but not in a dismissive way. "We do have pretty good screening for breast cancer," she said. I would have alternating mammograms and MRIs every six months, unless she found a lump or I chose to have my breasts removed. It's the ovarian cancer, my risk multiplied to about 20 percent, that no one would be able to find early enough. I'd have to get my ovaries out in my forties.

I've had my breasts poked and massaged by doctors since I was about twelve. They are impossible for me to examine at home, because between my dense tissue, family history of fibroids, and anxiety, I find scary pea-sized bumps everywhere. I don't trust my fingers, my breasts, or my mind, and I was delighted to have the director smashing my breast tissue under her hands. Security awaited me on the other side of the exam. I'd sit up, pull off my hospital gown, put my bra back on, and head home with a note to come back in six months.

Dr. Modesitt brought both hands to the top of my right breast, the pads of her fingers dancing around twelve o'clock. "Hm, I'm not sure," she said. "Feel right there." She took my fingers, and I pretended to feel the thing her expert hands had detected.

"Do you have some time?"

"Sure." I wasn't actually thinking anything other than *What if it really is too late?* Cognitive behavioral therapy works best when the fear is irrational. Otherwise, it's telling someone to take a deep breath when their pants are on fire.

"Let me call down to Radiology and see if they can squeeze you in now."

Have you ever imagined all social norms flying out the window? What would our conversation have sounded like?

*Taylor, I don't know what I'm feeling. It could be a tumor.*

*I'm freaked out. Did I mention I'm pregnant? I have kids . . .*

Instead, I was all nods and "Sure, sounds good!" like I was waiting for a retail employee to see if another store carried the gray wash denim in petite.

"You can get dressed, and I'll be right back."

Across the street in the west wing of the hospital, a woman with a bright tattooed arm sleeve carefully squeezed my breasts between clear plastic bookends and told me to hold my breath. I could have a mammogram while pregnant but not an MRI. Suddenly I became angry with this baby I wasn't even sure existed. I'd only taken home pregnancy tests. Yet there was a chance she was already keeping doctors from finding a malignancy.

I'd let my sisters deliver the news to my mom. I didn't have the wherewithal to join her in questioning whether the results of Tophs's tests were accurate. It was her right to consider the possibility of human error, whether as an outgrowth of hope or denial. But I had seen the results and sat down with Shelley. This wasn't a fluke.

Months later, my mom would get tested in Ohio for the BRCA2 mutation and receive positive results. She'd wonder if Tophs was a sort of angel, delivering a message that could save one (or many) of us. It was a thought I couldn't outright reject.

As Tophs grew older, he evoked a certain quality—a spiritual or sixth sense. He was dialed into emotions and the things people didn't say. As I sat on the couch one day, tired and pregnant, he held my face with both hands and stared into my eyes without a word. Tophs saw me. More than one friend asked me if he was a little prophet. They sorta laughed when they said it, but they weren't exactly joking. They giggled because we don't think of scrawny boys born in 2012 as modern John the Baptists. Tophs might not eat honey and locusts or preach to strangers in the wilderness, but I wouldn't count him out. He has an awareness that will never show up on a report card or genetic panel. He shares with those closest to him a quiet *knowing* that needs no diagnosis. While *prophet* is a mysterious word, people who observed Tophs weren't making a scary, end-of-times suggestion. They were human beings perceiving that quite possibly, wrapped in a fragile and complicated and dancing body, existed an expression of God we were privileged to behold.

Also wrapped in his body was a mutation that we couldn't change but at least had time to watch. Even if it was too late for me, maybe not for my mother or sisters. Maybe not for Tophs and his siblings and their kids.

The woman with tattoos led me back to the waiting room, where I sat in my pants and a gown that opened in the front. I assumed they'd read the scan and let me go. Instead, I was called into a dark room with a table and ultrasound machine. A middle-aged doctor with reddish hair and a warm smile, who also happened to run the UVA Breast Care program, walked in. They'd brought another director to me. This was all happening so fast.

"There were some white spaces on your mammogram, so I

just want to take a closer look," she said, lubing what resembled a computer mouse.

I no longer felt safe. What did she see? She said something about my tissue, about a spot her fingers could feel. And I wish I could tell you what happened next, but I don't know. Either she used terms I didn't understand or I was so panicked that I couldn't hear, but I left the room, the office, the hospital, still wondering what she'd found. My main question, the one I'd held so long for Tophs was *Should I be concerned?* It's tied to another. *Are you concerned?*

Usually that *you* is someone in a white coat. Sometimes it's Paul. I don't dare ask God, do I? If I asked God and he were to answer yes, what then? What if the one who held mountains in his hands wept over my test results? How could I be safe within the hands of that God?

I left the hospital and began sliding toward depression, heavy with the ambiguity of my first high-risk appointment. Paul relieved some of the stress by helping me make a plan. I would call after the weekend with a short list of questions. I did, and the director herself returned my call the same day. She told me not to worry. The image of my breast was negative, but because she felt something, as did Dr. Modesitt, I would see a breast surgeon. I was healthy, for the time being, yet everything had changed.

We walked along this new road—was it a detour or always the planned route—as a mother and her boy—one oblivious to danger or lack, the other shouldering parts of both bodies, hers and his, that no one could promise were healthy. I didn't have two working copies of a gene that suppresses tumors. If my one good copy were to mutate, for any long list of reasons, my lack, or genetic vulnerability, would be the perfect soil for an abundance of abnormal cells. Even if genetics figured Tophs out one day—*genetics is moving so quickly*, Shelley said—I could already be gone.

# 17

That winter, as nausea and depression settled in, my friend Kaitlyn stopped by our house to build forts with the kids or leave a case of Mr. Pibb on the porch with a handwritten card. Often she tucked a poem inside about Advent, her favorite season, one filled with hopeful waiting for a world without darkness.

I'd met Kaitlyn at a neighborhood cookout months before, but we'd really connected over frozen yogurt one afternoon when she told me she'd shadowed Shelley. Even though Charlottesville is a two-degrees-of-separation town, where you see your doctor at Trader Joe's and the Trader Joe's guy at the gym, I couldn't believe the coincidence. Kaitlyn, a heart failure patient in her twenties, would need a transplant eventually, but no one knew when. The genetics team hadn't found a cause for her cardiomyopathy, but she'd been so drawn to their knowledge and care for her that she was considering a career switch to genetic counseling.

I'd never met such a young and nonscary Christian so ready for Jesus to return. Kaitlyn was fed up with brokenness, with the ways our bodies let us down, yet she kept living. Kept hiding in the same cabinet over and over again until my kids caught on and found her, kept hanging Christmas lights inside forts and handing out Welch's fruit snacks at every visit.

Soon after Shelley had called, I'd sat down with Kaitlyn in the corner booth of a pizza shop and explained the BRCA results. She'd ordered an IPA, and I drank a Pibb on ice, and it was obvious by the way she listened and asked the right questions that this new friend was well acquainted with life lived in the middle.

The following spring, I finally agreed to leave the house again for more than five minutes. She promised she knew just the thing to lift my spirits. I climbed into her car, an old burgundy sedan she called the Chariot, and we drove five or ten minutes and parked on a street near the back of the hospital. As we crossed to a parking garage and neared the stairs, she shoved the midsized watermelon she carried under her sweatshirt. "There," she smirked, "we're twins."

"Who do you think the cops are gonna go after if we get caught?" I couldn't stop looking around, thinking about what might happen to Paul's job if we were found out. I'd never even streaked the Lawn as an undergrad. "They'll escort *you* home." Kaitlyn is white.

"Taylor, it'll be fine. Wait, are those cameras?" She grinned, and I was annoyed at her privilege but envious of the attitude that led her to water-ski with heart failure or chase a hefty dose of diuretics with a double shot of espresso.

I was willing to give Kaitlyn's crazy idea a chance because the girl had been wheeled into more surgeries and heart catheterization labs than I could count. During a recent echocardiogram, a tech actually looked at the monitor and said, "Whoa, I don't know how you're still walking around."

I knew she stood on the roof of that garage for me. But maybe she was there for herself too. For the person who would have to die one day in order for her to live. For what it meant to live in bodies that can betray us, bodies designed by a God we believe is fully loving, holy, and near.

We reached the side that backed up to trees. A sidewalk ran along the garage on the ground level.

"What if someone walks out right when I drop it?"

"Taylor, no one is here."

That wasn't exactly true. There were cars parked on each level, just not many. And we'd seen a few souls on the drive in.

*Pregnant woman injures passerby while trying to unwind.*

"Fine, drop it over there." She pointed to an area, a mix of straw and grass and dirt. "But wait a second."

I turned, sure a cop was behind us.

"I want you to think of the most frustrating and upsetting things about the last few months. Get those in your head first."

I paused. Test results. Nonanswers. Puking. Carrying a mutation I couldn't change or chase from my kids.

I picked up the watermelon, felt the weight of this fruit born of a seed, and launched it, with both hands, up and over and into the air. I do not recall its short flight, how fast it sank or stayed whole. I only remember we got what we wanted: the quick splat of insides exposed, a thing undone right before our eyes, and the rush of satisfaction that warmed me from my stomach to my ears.

A lightness I hadn't felt in months.

"Next time," she said, "we'll drop a pumpkin over pavement."

## 18

It was a morning like every weekday morning: Paul and I rushing to get our preschoolers fed, dressed, and in the van to attend two different schools. Tophs, as usual, wanted time on the computer. I did a quick back and forth in my head, weighing the cons of screen time against the pro of putting on my underwear in peace. *Screw it, he'll live.* I left him to click away on the mouse.

I half watched, half listened to make sure he wasn't watching explicit videos on YouTube or climbing atop the leaning bookcase. But I also needed to get dressed, see what Eliot's curls were doing, and grab her a headband. She could pick out her own clothes in pre-K, usually a dress or leggings and a tutu with a sequined headband and Pumas. She dressed much louder than she acted at school, her clothes, perhaps, saying the words she kept in her belly.

I could overhear Tophs saying, "Uh huh, yes, that's it! There we go!" The kid who couldn't tell me when he was hungry had navigated from the screensaver to Amazon by accessing previously viewed websites. "There we go!" he said again. That should have been warning enough.

I was impressed by this three-year-old's willingness to jump into an activity and experiment without knowing where he'd end up. Eliot has always wanted instruction before engaging a task. She and I want to know there's a right path we can follow. Tophs couldn't always tell you what he was doing, but that brain of his was working in ways mine never has. He was happy, I was unbothered, and I gave him a few more minutes alone before we left for school.

Later that day, I checked my email and found several new notices from Amazon, confirming receipt of my orders. Paul and I share an account, so I didn't think much of it. But as I clicked on the emails and opened my order history, I saw items I had no words for: two leather Rebecca Minkoff cross-body handbags—one white with tassels, the other turquoise—totaling $370.33. I checked our bank account. The money was gone. And there was more: a seven-inch Amazon Fire tablet, along with three chargers, for $99.98. I fired off emails, explaining my three-year-old son had ordered the purses. The sellers were really nice when they told me, "Sorry, but it's already been processed for shipping."

I couldn't ask Tophs what he'd done. I would have been met with those eyes. At pick-up, Paige and I joked that maybe he'd ordered the bags as an early Mother's Day gift. The story was funny, but also a boost—evidence that my boy was smart and capable. He had just started saying his own name, but if we could avoid major hypoglycemic episodes with snacks, maybe he could be on grade level by kindergarten.

Paige mentioned this possibility at one of our first IEP meetings. An IEP, or Individualized Education Program, is both a written plan and a program that includes the special education services and accommodations a kid like Tophs needs—and is promised by law—in order to thrive. In preschool, a classroom teacher and case manager, speech and language pathologist, and occupational therapist worked together to help Tophs. The IEP team also includes the parents, a fact that Paige never needed to be reminded of.

Ideally, every educator would make room for the nuance of Tophs's situation—the fact that, outside of hypoglycemia, language disorders, and developmental delays, we lacked a clear diagnosis, a word that bound these things together. They would recognize the unknown physiological elements that likely affect his engagement, processing speed, and overall mood. They would ask "What more could we be doing for this child?" instead of "What's the least we can do under the law?"

That's how the IEP process started for us. Paul and I would walk into Paige's classroom; she'd turn to greet us with a big smile, an open can of Diet Coke on her desk. "Come on in!" Tophs would hurry off to the sensory table or play kitchen, smacking down fake food on fake appliances. Meanwhile, Paul and I sat in small plastic chairs at a low table across from Paige, the mood less like a board meeting and more like chatting with a neighbor.

"He's doing great," she'd often say. She shared stories of his growth, benchmarks he'd met, but also what still puzzled her. Paige kept working with him during one-on-one time until the shapes and colors on flashcards brought words from Tophs's lips. She constantly reminded us of his strengths in a way that didn't make us feel silly to have concerns. "What do you think?" or "What do you see at home?" she'd ask. She wasn't afraid to veer off the page, to set the papers down and listen. Or to try new ways to engage him—would spinning him in a swing help his processing speed? Would holding a fidget toy make him less anxious? Would he enjoy the input of a weighted blanket? Could he benefit from spending circle time with more typically developing peers each morning?

Paige wouldn't let Tophs slip. Even while I read through every goal on his IEP and we stopped to ask questions, my overall sense was: Tophs is in the best hands. Maybe he'd overcome his delays and start elementary school with no strings or services attached, just a short, giggling kid with a clean slate.

I left those early meetings secure in my belief that Paige and the rest of her team weren't afraid to *see* Tophs. Sitting there, across from someone I could trust, the educator who had first understood our daughter and now our son, I made a critical mistake: I conflated special education and the IEP process with one exceptional woman. And I assumed we wouldn't leave her side until Tophs finished preschool.

# 19

Exactly eight months after Shelley's phone call, I gave birth in that same crunchy hospital to our third baby, who was, in fact, a girl. We named her Juliet, and she looked and weighed more like her sister Eliot than her brother Tophs. Paul and I were officially outnumbered, and I daydreamed about naps and the golden days when my breasts didn't leak without permission.

People are always talking about being pregnant with an idea, but you can deliver a big idea—you can, say, start a business—without an episiotomy. I won't say Paul was pregnant with a church, but even before he started seminary, we knew he would eventually pastor. The son of a preacher man would become a preacher. Even before we married, I knew this calling on Paul's life was true and good. It existed somewhere out there, beyond his PhD and years as a high school counselor, and I wanted him to answer the call one day. I never even considered turning away.

As Paul finished night and weekend seminary at a neck-breaking pace, we thought he might join the staff of a local church. He didn't need to be senior pastor, like his dad and grandfather had been. But the more time we spent serving in local congregations, the more we couldn't see ourselves there indefinitely. We loved the traditional Black Baptist church for what it represented, but the confines of tradition and denomination proved too restrictive for me. And a large white evangelical church in town, where we were loved by people who loved Jesus and conservatism, couldn't speak to being Black in America. We grew tired of seeing the same "brothers" and "sisters" who greeted us on Sunday post racist Facebook updates throughout the week.

I remember one of my old college friends sitting on our living room couch, listening and nodding, innately understanding our position: we wanted to serve the Lord but also felt stuck. "Start your own church," she said. I told her to shut her mouth.


Less than two months after Juliet was born, we visited our former church in northern Virginia for Paul's birthday. What a righteous dude, wanting church as his present. It was the church we'd attended before moving to Charlottesville in 2011, a place where it wasn't uncommon to see several Black people, even different groups of Black people, gathering at one time—a luxury Charlottesville had afforded us just once every two years during UVA's Black Alumni weekend.

So we packed up the kids one morning in September and drove to the large sanctuary, where a full band and group of singers led us in worship, the spotlights operated by a different team in the back. And as I looked toward the stage, I just knew. A shift in my belly, a hum in my chest, a whisper only I heard. We'd come back. Paul still worked full-time at UVA as an assistant professor in the school of education. Our two older kids, one with special needs, were settled in school. I had just entered a high-risk screening program at a research-driven hospital. Tophs's doctors and therapists were based in Charlottesville. How could I explain his medical records to a new pediatrician? Moving didn't make any practical sense at the time. How do you calculate the distance between an out-there-somewhere idea and reality?

"We're going to move," I told Paul when we got in the van to drive home.

"You think so?" he asked with a half smile. A boy eager to follow a dream, a grown man anchored by prayer and prudence.

Paul and the senior pastor of the church developed a possible plan. We'd relocate to northern Virginia for about two years while Paul joined the staff and still worked at UVA. After he trained alongside other pastors, we'd return to Charlottesville to start a church. *Church plant* is the evangelical term.

We both prayed; we both knew, without a doubt, we had to go. Even if it didn't make sense. I think Paul could put some of the pieces together in his head, in an *I'll make it work* way. But I can't think of another time in my life when I've been so perplexed by what I believed was right. So certain of this thing I couldn't understand. Was that faith?

Eliot's kindergarten teacher, who had carefully and patiently allowed our quiet girl to ease into the classroom, teared up when we told her we were moving in December, right in the middle of the school year. "As an educator, I know better," Paul said.

Paige, sad to lose Tophs from her class, said she'd seen it coming—maybe not the move but the ministry—and believed we'd be back.

"We'll be back," I kept saying, a way of declaring that this wouldn't be hard, or permanent, that nothing would be lost.

I love Paul in all the ways. For his pragmatic thinking, for leaving that rose on my door in college, for buying me a pair of Pumas in Times Square when my feet hurt from wearing boots, for crying as he told his mom they'd taken our firstborn to the NICU for some TLC. I wanted this for him. I've never personally felt the call to pastor, but the man I love was born to care for people in this way. I could write and mother anywhere. We'd make it work. We set a date to move the week before Christmas.


The weeks before we moved dragged along in a strange parade of doctor's appointments, the hospital lobby a living room I crossed each morning. First, a consultation with the breast surgeon, whose nurse asked, "So you don't actually have a problem, per se?" as she checked me in.

*I don't know, do I?*

The surgeon herself was not warm and fuzzy, but I instantly trusted her. Dark hair fell neatly around her face, and she sat, leaning forward, as she listened to my story. Tophs; the results given the same day I tested positive for Juliet; the lack of breast and ovarian cancer in my family tree.

"I see patients with mutations all the time, but this is kind of crazy. I don't want to make you feel odd, but if you're having a hard time wrapping your mind around this, it's understandable." And this, a balm for my soul: "This came out of left field for you."

If I chose to have a prophylactic mastectomy, this woman would be the one to take my breasts apart, to check my incisions the morning after. She couldn't tell me what to do—no one would ever tell me to have my breasts removed precancer. But I wanted, more than anything, for her to *tell me what to do.*

Next, at the plastic surgery consult, I sat in a sterile room with a man I'd just met, a surgery resident or fellow, looking at pictures of women's bare breasts on his camera. Juliet, still young enough to sleep through everything but the night, hadn't stirred once in her car seat on the floor next to me. I might make it through the visit without having to be mom *and* patient.

"Do you know if you'll want to save your nipples?" He meant as opposed to tossing them and having new ones tattooed.

How many weeks had passed since I'd learned nipple tattoos were a thing? Four. How long since I'd first traced my family pedigree, searching for ovarian or breast or pancreatic cancer in close range—and come up empty? A year.

"Dr. Modesitt recommended the tattoos. She thought they would look better." Were these *my* words? Did I have a gynecologic oncologist at a cancer center?

He clicked through the side-by-side photos, pointing out scars, spared nipples, even elaborate star-like designs inked over chests. I could hear the commercial in my head: *Why stop at a nipple when you can have the whole sky?* He told me some women have tissue taken from the abdomen instead of getting implants. He wasn't sure, judging by my size, if I had enough fat to make that an option. I found way too much joy in that.

Then I stood topless by the door as the surgeon took my naked mugshot for future reference, if I decided to schedule a surgery. "Hmm, your breasts are more pendulimic," he said.

Kaitlyn and I had a saying for when something happened, either serious or dumb, that pushed us over the edge: TAR. That's About Right. As in, you have up to an 86 percent lifetime risk of getting breast cancer and, oh, by the way, your boobies are dangly. TAR. If Kaitlyn's latest cardiac labs didn't look good and then a guitar-playing youth group leader asked her out after church, TAR.

I left with a page or two of notes in a black Moleskine, where I kept a paper from Shelley tucked in the back. A year ago, she'd mapped out my genetic pedigree. She'd drawn circles and squares, some shaded, some crossed through, and lines connecting them. It was less of a family tree and more of a grid, really. This paper had become a trail guide, marking life and death and, by omission, highlighting the space where I now lived. It told me things I hadn't asked to learn and didn't tell me what I needed to know, like if I should have surgery and how I should talk to my children one day about me, about them.

Kaitlyn met me in the hallway between her office, where she assisted Shelley and other genetic counselors, and my next stop, the children's hospital, where Paul had taken Tophs for his first echocardiogram. One of the variants found through whole exome sequencing had been linked, in some cases, to a disease that can affect the heart.

"Are you okay?" she asked.

"How are you doing?" Dr. Marcus Potter had asked.

"Yeah, I'm fine."

"I don't think you are, Taylor," Kaitlyn said. I held the baby, and Kaitlyn held my purse, leading the way, so that we wouldn't have to walk outside in the cold, so that I wouldn't feel a thing.

Tophs was shirtless on an exam table, as someone pulled stickers and nodes off his chest. Kaitlyn waved hello and went back to work. And I thought I was present, I knew I was the mother, but when the round and friendly cardiologist arrived, I heard him say that Tophs was in trouble. That the echo was not clear, that he was at risk, that we should bring him in any time his blood sugar drops and have his heart monitored in the ER.

Paul, clear-eared and calm, told me later what the doctor had actually said: The echo looked good. He wasn't worried about Tophs. We could bring him back in a couple of years.

Who am I and where am I and what, even, is dangerous?

That same week, I pumped milk in an exam room at the UVA breast care center so that my breasts would be empty for a mammogram. My phone rang; another genetic counselor, one who specifically worked with adults and cancer patients, was on the other end.

"Hi, Mrs. Harris, is this a good time to talk?"

The breast surgeon had asked her to take a look at my case.

"Yep, just finished up pumping." I stood, half-naked, half-dripping, trying to take coherent notes.

"I've been looking at your family history, and I don't know if the type of cancers we see, like uterine and stomach, can be explained by your BRCA2 mutation. There could be a second gene mutation in your family."

What in the lactating hell?

"You wouldn't have to do additional genetic testing right away, but I think your family history is suspicious enough to warrant more testing if you want."

Another mutation could mean more screenings or preventive measures to protect me from other forms of cancer, like colon or uterine or cervical, which were part of my family history. In a way, the counselor's words were everything I'd wanted—the security that searching for an answer wasn't over the top. But I didn't feel the way I'd imagined I would. I told her about my friend Lindsay, how she'd preempted the cancer that had affected so many women in her family with a double mastectomy.

"I think your family history is harder in some ways because it's not clear cut."

I noticed the tech in the doorway, and as we got ready to hang up, she said, "It's not a guarantee you'll get it, but a *risk*."

The only guarantee is I am high risk.

The only guarantee is that we don't know.

# 20

Our move could not be measured in the hundred miles between Charlottesville and northern Virginia. We settled in a county outside Washington, D.C., where farmland has lost out to McMansions, and where Teslas, as well as an overwhelming sense of entitlement, abound. The shift was enormous, the pace of life too quick, the thinking not progressive enough, and, outside of church, the empathy too scarce. I grew up as one of the have-nots in a wealthy suburb, so I didn't feel a need to keep up with the Joneses. The abundance of wealth didn't necessarily unsettle me. It was the paucity of knowledge of best practices among educators that I couldn't understand, given our proximity to D.C. and the twenty-first century.

After just one IEP meeting in our new school district, I understood why many parents loathe them. Sometimes you walk into a cold, sterile room and sit across from people who must have once loved *something* about their job but have become dull to new stories and students. They've traded ideas and innovation for rote phrases.

Tophs played on the floor, Paul sat to my left, and I held Juliet, six months old, in my lap. A woman with short blonde hair and thick mascara, who had worked in central administration for umpteen years, began the meeting for Tophs's transfer.

"We are recommending three days a week for Christopher." She'd been called in to lay down the law.

"But he attends school five days a week in Charlottesville," Paul said. "You haven't even had a chance to work with him. What evidence are you basing your decision on?"

We naïvely thought they would accept the work of their colleagues two hours down the road and make adjustments later.

"Well, in *this* county . . ."

Never a good sign.

". . . we reserve the five-day-a-week spots for students with the most severe disabilities."

"Why is that? He's made great progress with early intervention. Why change that before you even meet him?" *Go, Paul, go, Paul!* I watched him defend our son's right to keep learning.

Her, looking at his transfer IEP, as our brown boy played with a model school bus on the floor and her teammates talked sweetly to the baby on my lap: "They gave him way too many speech hours."

"So you're saying you don't trust the judgment of your in-state colleagues, even though you have haven't worked with our son?" Paul wasn't yelling. He had to be firm but cordial, a professor who never made others feel threatened. He had to be father to a son he didn't always understand but whom he'd give up any job or degree for.

"I'm saying *this* is it." She tossed the papers down on the table. "This is what we're offering."

*Oooh, child.* I can be meek and lack confidence, I can be filled to the brim with social anxiety—until a room full of white people tell me I want too much. They suggested we take him to the library on the two days he wouldn't be in school. They treated us as though we were looking for free childcare, not a continuation of services.

I let Paul lead the rebuttal. He provided the structure, I filled in with details of Toplis's history. I don't think they knew what to make of us. We are middle class. We are highly educated. We are Christians. Yet we weren't overcome with gratitude when one teacher offered, "Some kids don't even go to school until kindergarten!"

*Really?* How dare we demand our son receive what is secured by law. This is how Black students, in particular, are railroaded by the American education system every single day.

Whenever my therapist asks me how I'm feeling, I have to look at an emotions cheat sheet. I've never fit the stereotype of the talkative emotional wife who wants to verbally process while her husband watches football. I'd rather find a good book in a dimly lit cave.

But I know anger, and a righteous rage burned in my gut. My son wouldn't be another who slipped through the cracks of the system or was pushed off a cliff.

As I opened my mouth to share one last comment, my rage

disintegrated. My voice cracked. I looked down, but I couldn't make my tears retreat. I willed myself to keep it together as the people who'd worked so hard to push us away scrambled to hand me tissues.

"I just want to say that this didn't have to be so hard." Behind those words were tests they knew nothing of. Behind those words were twenty thousand genes with a handful of confusing and upending mutations. Behind those words was an astute doctor who said, "He's got something; we just aren't smart enough to figure it out yet." They had no idea. And they didn't ask. They didn't care.

We refused to sign. Which meant Tophs would sit out of school for at least two weeks until we reconvened. The kid who we knew was a poster child for early intervention would stay at home because someone in a position of power had reasoned, without knowing him, that he should have less.

You can leave an IEP meeting feeling any range of emotions. My friend, also mom to a child with special needs, says she and her husband usually take the whole day off from work and grab burgers and shakes after their long, stressful meetings. Even meetings that aren't particularly contentious can leave you drained, walking around in what I call the "IEP haze."

Around that time, I developed the mental hashtag #NotMyBlackBoy. I would repeat it in my head as I prepared to engage educators who would try to convince me that in Tophs's case, the bare bones would do. As Tophs's mother, I'm never just advocating for an undiagnosed child whose challenges don't follow any script; I'm also a Black mother advocating for my Black son in a room full of people who don't look like us. With an education gap between races that lingers at the threshold of almost every school building you step foot in, I have to hold both these truths close.

I agonized over what the team said about us when we weren't in the room. I'd prefer to compliment a teacher's ballet flats and sign on the dotted line. But Paul and I know too much. As much as these frustrating meetings are about advocating for a child whose root condition is unknown, they also are about fighting for a child whose race *is* known, whose trajectory cannot be determined by people who don't care to know him.

Perhaps no one else in the room is consciously thinking about race. But Paul and I play a game called "Can you imagine?" A game in which we consider the situation and change the race of the person involved. It's how we might think about a white terrorist being escorted to Burger King by cops. *Can you imagine if that had been a brutha?* Or an unarmed man being shot six times in his back for holding a cell phone. *They would've taken a white man to Burger King.* In less lethal scenarios, it might be picturing a white professor at a top-tier university being told, when he expressed concern about his son's processing speed, that he should take his son on vacation, point out the birds and the sand. He should, like, *talk* to him. Or it's wondering if a white mother with degrees from UVA and Johns Hopkins, when noting her son's history of sensory-related challenges, would be told, "We all have sensory needs, you know. Like, sometimes I need to get up and walk around."

And what happens when a single parent working two jobs walks into a meeting? Or a parent who is stressed about making rent or has another child with more urgent needs? What then?

But because my allegiance is to God and not to white people maintaining the status quo, I also wondered if this move had been some cosmic misunderstanding. I kept thinking about Abraham offering up Isaac, an angel intercepting the human sacrifice—I didn't want to offer up our boy in order to start a church in Charlottesville. I didn't want that to be what God required, but what if it were? What if we didn't get the Happy Meal version of answering God's call? While I felt called to northern Virginia for a short time, I couldn't make practical sense of the sacrifice. Did Paul's apprenticeship—training church members to lead Bible studies, or attending staff meetings, or even preaching sermons in back-to-back-to-back services on Sundays—necessitate loss for our family? Paul will always be a people person, a pastor's pastor, the guy other ministers pull aside to share their burdens with. And I wanted him there, ready to listen and care for others. On one hand, I said, "Whatever you want, Jesus," and on the other hand, "Don't you see us? Can't you help Tophs? Don't forget him, God." A tired mother's psalm. Maybe it's because I'm the youngest child or have bought into prosperity-driven Western Christianity. Whatever the reason, I wanted it both ways. I would not lose my son to eighteen months of poor education in his most critical years of development.

At the next meeting, the gatekeeper from central admin relented, agreeing to let Tophs attend preschool five days a week. But later that spring, the team reproposed three days a week of school, and, once again, we refused to sign. Thankfully, the law works in parents' favor in such cases, and the team reverts to the last agreed-upon document.

When trying to bargain us down, a team member would remind us that the IEP was amendable. In other words, if Tophs started to fall far enough away from average, then they would consider adding services back. Try telling that to Paul, a former high school counselor in that same county, who served students who'd been overlooked or underserved for years until it was too late—until their options were far more limited than they needed to be. That would not be our son.

The loss, for everyone involved in such IEP meetings, can be measured in time, energy, and imagination. When my concerns about Tophs are ignored or referred to in air quotes, as though only hard numbers matter, we all lose. What angers me most as a mother is that I have to be deficit-oriented in meetings to get my point across. If I commend Tophs's progress and strengths, they will think I'm agreeing to cut his services. How is it that a system operates without space for a parent to recognize strengths *and* pinpoint needs? At what point did efficiency kill nuance?

In one meeting, my observation finally seemed to make a difference. When discussing Tophs's ability to retrieve words we know he's learned, I shared a story of him recalling an injury at school. "I fell and there was that red stuff on my shirt. What's that red thing called?" he'd asked.

A pause. His ability to find the word *blood* hung in the air between us. Their faces softened.

I wondered if Tophs sensed the resistance within the county we'd felt as his parents. For the first time since he'd started school as a two-year-old, he complained about going. He'd rather be home building elaborate two-story barns with magnetic tiles for his growing herd of My Little Ponies.

At home in our rented condo, Tophs worked carefully and quietly, and he didn't want help. He had the vision. My brown, curly-haired architect with hands that struggled to button but balanced triangles until they clicked together to form the square panel of a wall.

"Look, Mommy!" I didn't dare touch. But I took it in. This was his area of mastery, a place he could retreat to and revel in strength and ability. Perhaps all he'd wanted from the start, even years before as a toddler, was a place he could feel capable and safe. Was that all I'd wanted too?

"Wow, Tophs! I love how creative you are. You've worked so hard." I tried to say all the right things. "Is this a *stable*?" He didn't care about my farm vocabulary, the way I tried to slip it in like spinach into meatloaf.

"Look, they're sleeping," he said, pointing to Fluttershy or Pinkie Pie or Twilight Sparkle resting on their hooves. His voice always raspy, the way an old wooden fence feels against your palm. I can't remember when the ponies, raised from the dead of my eighties childhood, found their way into Tophs's life, but I'm convinced they will never leave. Their cosmic eyes don't scare him, and he doesn't seem to mind when a kid laughs at him for bringing one to church. They give him words and characters and templates for conversation.

"I don't like it! I *love* it!" He stole from Pinkie Pie, the pony who shoots streamers from a portable cannon. Alone but befriended in this world of figurines, Tophs directs the magic and sets the scenes. He improvises; *his* ponies travel to Target to buy even more ponies, but even if the ponies disagree or one falls prey to feathered bangs cut with blunt-tip scissors, the theme remains the same: *Friendship is Magic*.

Sometimes I worried whether Tophs connected with kids his age, especially as he left the self-contained special education preschool classroom and entered kindergarten in a new school with typically developing peers. He still received academic, speech, and occupational therapy services, but he mostly learned alongside kids who didn't need that sort of targeted help. I tried not to obsess over the fact that he went to class with kids who attended after-school learning programs to "get ahead." I'd go crazy gathering lack if I followed my racing type-A thoughts down that trail.

"I'm in love with Cori," he announced one evening at dinner. "She's sooo sweet. She said I'm cute. I telled a little bit of my friends I'm in love with Cori." Maybe I had no reason to worry.

Cori, his classmate, had long, wavy hair like the ponies Tophs adored, and the two attended a speech group together. Tophs had probably been crushing on her for a while; earlier in the year, he mentioned Cori had told him to get away from her. I couldn't tell whether this was regular playground stuff or if Tophs had been constantly touching or nagging her, the way he sometimes did with me or his sisters. It came from an innocent place, but that wouldn't matter as he got older. Which is exactly the danger with Tophs: without a name for his condition or a great understanding of how he processes information, I've imagined future social situations that could be particularly perilous for him.

Imagine a young Black man, who isn't an auditory processor, who doesn't always know where his body is in space, who would stand in the middle of a road if he thought someone might need help, who isn't diabetic but is hypoglycemic, who will become clammy and heavy as stone if he misses a meal, having a run-in with a police officer.

Is he distracted by the flashing lights? If he hasn't been pulled over before, can he process what this means, get to the side of the road quickly enough without striking a match of resentment within the cop? Will he, like his father, know how to keep his hands on the steering wheel? There is no visual to tell him what to do. Who will remind him to say, "Good evening, Officer. My registration is in the glove compartment. May I reach over?"

So many ways it could go wrong in a flash. I don't know how to tell you about the intersection of these burdens—Black and undiagnosed—in a world that is comfortable with neither.

Elijah McClain, twenty-three, dancing along the street in Colorado one summer, playing his violin for cats in a shelter, then apologizing to officers as they clamped his artery and shut off the valve to his life. I couldn't stop crying when I read of Elijah. Out of everyone on that List, he most closely resembles my son. Happy and empathic, eccentric and rhythmic. He deserved space here, was worthy to wear his face mask, whether to keep warm from anemia or safe from social anxiety or just because he liked it.

"He had a child-like spirit," his friend April Young said in an article for *The Cut*. "He lived in his own little world. He was never into, like, fitting in. He just was who he was."

My son in his world of ponies, dancing to Common and John Legend's "Glory," cradling my face in his tiny hands.

"I thank God that he was my son because just him being born brought life into my world, you know what I mean?" Elijah's mother said. "I know he was giving life to other people too."

He gave life, they took his. No mother deserves to stand in the place where these two truths meet.

21

I was under no illusion that Charlottesville, a place I've found undeniably gorgeous, was set apart from the rest of America. Still, I didn't see them coming. The first time our family was rattled in a new way, a too-near way, by racism, occurred during our first summer away from Charlottesville, on August 11, 2017. The day *Charlottesville* became shorthand for the worst, yet inevitable, fruit of seeing Black people as fractions.

I should have known. When I lived on Jefferson's Lawn and heard a drunk student yell outside about *niggers* taking all the white women, I should have calculated, to the decimal point, to the date and hour, when the fruit of his lips would ripen, mature into hideous, widespread rot. On a Friday night, sixteen years after I shuddered in my room, wishing for a deadbolt lock, fresh white boys in T-shirts and polos, in denim and khakis, carried the flaming torches of their forefathers and tore across the Lawn with entitled abandon. They trampled the grass where I'd walked and lived as a fourth-year student, the place where my love had proposed with rose petals and songs, the place where I'd taken a picture of Eliot as a barely sitting babe in front of my old room. They beat back bodies there without restraint as cops and authorities stood down for the nightmarish ticker-tape parade of rage-wrapped privilege. *Like begets like.*

The next day, a white man, not a lone wolf, drove his car into people made in the image of God, whose organs and bones and feet had worked until the point when tons of metal whipped them into a bloody meringue.

We watched that scene from our family room in northern Virginia, wanting to be home in Charlottesville, not understanding why this would happen when we were away. We had not moved to hide or escape. Paul needed to train as an associate pastor in an established church to increase the chances his church plant would last longer than six months or reach beyond the walls of our house. But the timing seemed all wrong—how could we return to a city and minister grace and peace when we'd been absent for the worst moments?

As a family, we traveled to Charlottesville for appointments at least once or twice a month, and Paul made the trip several times a week for classes and faculty meetings. Never once did I wonder, *How could this happen in Charlottesville?* At least not in the way the bumper stickers with cute hearts and the city's name might have you think. Charlottesville was not some beacon of justice, a city on a hill infiltrated by radicals. As a parent, though, I did wonder *how.* As in how could the place where my daughter's sandals slapped across cobblestone as she ate ice cream become an avenue of death less than forty-eight hours later? It was curious in the way a terminally ill person is living and breathing, and then suddenly not. Not in the way a professional might inspect a house, judge the foundation solid, and the very next day find the house has sunken into the ground. Charlottesville, while beautiful, is America, and America, at its core, is Charlottesville. The foundation is not firm, but we hold up the papers, saying, "Look, it is written . . ." as though the men who wrote and signed the papers were God and not idols of privilege.

Paul and I stood, frozen, on August 12 as CNN moved the car forward again, and again. Our job in the moment was not to speak to those arguing, "This is not our sweet little town" and "This is not our great country." Our job was to find a way to explain these images to our children, all while sinking into that well-worn groove where Black adults go When This Sort of Thing Happens.

The careful counselor, Paul started the conversation with Eliot, who was six. We'd talked about her beautiful brown skin and thick, curly hair, and she had a sense for why Rosa had stayed seated and Dr. King was assassinated. But we'd never discussed anything this present, this evil, this close to home. Tophs, meanwhile, played alone, probably with his ponies.

Paul used the words *racism, Charlottesville, UVA, white people,* and *police.* And what happened next isn't fair. A burden folded itself over Eliot's shoulders, a mantle I didn't want her to carry, and she said, "Uh-oh. We're Black people." I could not bring her back.

"Is this gonna happen every day in Charlottesville?" she asked.

*Which part?* I wanted to ask. *The racism, the destruction of Black neighborhoods, the hidden pockets of public housing among great wealth? Yes. But a racist rally and car crash? No.*

As Tophs was playing, Eliot was learning norms, feeling her way through fear, wondering if she'd be next. She was just six. Her school supply list still called for blunt-tip scissors. I heard the terrorists hid weapons in bushes.

We had dinner plans that night, and as we got into the van, she murmured, "I just can't believe what happened in Charlottesville." She still conjugated some of her verbs incorrectly, and I didn't correct her when she said, "Is Mimi white or brown? Would they have foughted Mimi?" She wanted to know if her light-skinned grandmother would have been in harm's way. Look how the world opened like a pop-up book before her.

I listened as she processed by trying to explain it to her younger brother, her voice just as raspy as his: "Some white people don't like Black people. There were police cops that were really helpful and some that were not that helpful. So I can tell you more about it later." Tophs wouldn't give her the time of day. "I wanna go to Target," he said. In his mind, he still lived unburdened. Maybe as a result of his age or his developmental differences. He does not, we do not, live apart from the intersections. Race, meet Atypical Development. Whatever the cause, I accepted Tophs's indifference this time as mercy.

Nine days after the rally, we drove back to Charlottesville. I did not plan to visit the memorial to Heather Heyer. We were supposed to go to the Discovery Museum, eat lunch, and find glasses for the eclipse while Paul worked. But in order to visit the museum, we had to drive into the garage and over the pavement where white supremacists beat a Black man named Dre Harris with metal poles while he blacked out again and again.

Flanked by Tophs and Eliot, pushing Juliet in her stroller, I moved from the garage toward the mounds of dried flowers, signs, and once-dripping wax. I didn't even know if the kids should be there, but I couldn't walk another path. Eliot stared at the words chalked on brick walls and down the street, but Tophs jumped along the sidewalk, hopping the length of long-stemmed roses pressed flat by rain and grief. The baby babbled and kicked her chunky legs in the sun.

Someone, in all the words of hope and sorrow, had created a finish line of roses, perhaps marking where the car plowed into the crowd. Here, where his bumper tore into flesh, into those made in God's image that he hoped to destroy. Here, where we were supposed to start a church and bring people together. Racial reconciliation was one of the church's core values, but we didn't just want to hold hands with white people and sing songs. Was reconciliation even possible? Meaningful? Or had we already been defeated? We stood near the corner of Fourth and Water Streets. Faith, meet racism. Children, meet cynicism. Black children, understand your God is not a white man.

It would take another year for Tophs to dive into Black history. A teacher in Charlottesville let him borrow a copy of *Young, Gifted and Black*, and he took to it with a focus and passion I hadn't seen since he danced to "Glory." His uncanny ability to recall dates and page numbers and exact lines from the legends' profiles reminded me of wisdom Eliot once shared with me about her brother.

Eliot doesn't remember the first day we rushed Tophs to the ER. We don't usually say, "He has an IEP." We say, "That teacher helps Tophs learn certain things, like how you used to go to speech therapy." But she's intuitive, and she probably noticed ways that Tophs was just Tophs. Easter morning, as I drove the kids to the church in northern Virginia where Paul worked all three services, I started to explain why we celebrate the holiday. I went through the whole story—Jesus's death, the empty tomb. I finished, feeling really thorough, and Tophs responded with something completely irrelevant.

"Tophs, did you hear anything I just said?"

Eliot, quickly aging ten or fifteen years, said, "Mommy, it goes in his mind."

That's right. She would know. He's her little brother. They are separated sometimes by her anxiety or "big feelings," sometimes by his mysterious symptoms, and sometimes just by whatever separates any siblings only eighteen months apart.

# 22

M ommy, remember when you used to feed Juliet with your boobs?" asked Tophs.

"Yeah . . . ?"

"That was super cute."

Every time I wanted to properly worry about Tophs, he'd show me more of his incredible, hilarious self. By age five, Tophs hadn't outgrown his delays, but he talked and understood much more than the three-year-old who'd sat in Paige's circle time. He started reading in kindergarten and took off, moving on from pointing out the large red letters for his favorite store, Target, to reading two and three-syllable words. He'd learned his letters and their sounds, but I could never get him to sound words out, the way Mom taught me and I'd taught Eliot with small books of laminated notecards. I think he trapped the words, sucked them into his memory, and did his best when he came across a word he'd never seen.

He never stopped dancing or singing—but he began singing with vibrato. And, of course, he could never have too much screen time. If something good came out of our time in northern Virginia schools, it wasn't so much that Tophs changed as a person, it was that we got to see more of him. We were now privy to Tophs, and learning him was a mystery and delight. In addition to the comedic faces, we got entire comedic phrases that trended among our family and friends.

One of the first was "Look to my leggies." We had no idea what it meant. Tophs would point both forefingers in one direction, "Look to my leggies," and then point the other way, repeat it, and laugh. It caught like fire. I could be talking to Paul about anything, from writing to a dinner recipe I botched, and he'd turn to me and say, "Oh yeah? Well, look to my leggies."

Whether he means to or not, Tophs captures an idea or emotion and packages it in a way that seems organic, as though he just dropped in to reveal what's always been true. Like the time he pointed to my sagging breasts and declared, "Plimpsies!" He was right. They were, indeed, plimpsies.

Sometimes he embodied the sass of TV characters. While I'll never understand why My Little Pony has been Tophs's long-lasting obsession, I can see how he came to relish Bartleby, the indigo smart-aleck cat on the Netflix series *True and the Rainbow Kingdom*. The show is trippy, but Bartleby is a study in deadpan humor. One day when Eliot and Tophs were playing Legos, I overheard her scolding him: "Tophs! Don't put your people in my pool yet! I just built it. I need to make it more sturdy."

"*Sturdy* is not even a thing, of course," he replied. It's this targeted sass that could give him confidence at a dinner party years from now or be harnessed to protect him from kids on the play-ground. Other times, he borrowed exact lines from characters. "I'm not ready to be a mom!" he announced to our family one night. I looked at Paul. What in the world? Then it clicked. The kids had recently watched *The Star*, an animated film about Jesus's birth. Tophs was the Virgin Mary.

Another time, angry at Paul in a restaurant, he yelled from the booth, "You're not my dad!" I couldn't stop laughing. He was quoting a line from *Annie*, starring Quvenzhané Wallis. He used this line again and again during the *Annie* phase when he didn't want to go potty. He'd even add, "I'm not an orphan. I'm a fos-ter kid!"

The timing of his *Annie* lines told us he identified with the character's emotion. Her words became a vessel for his frustration or sense of betrayal. I don't know if that's a life hack, but for a kid who sometimes struggles to find words, I saw it as a win, Tophs's version of texting a GIF.

His ability to improvise, to combine a new situation with mem-orized quotes, to weave in and out of fiction and real life with such control was remarkable. We were riding in the minivan one day when Tophs called up from the backseat. "Is there something you wanna tell me, *Paul*?" He'd been testing boundaries lately, feeling out the rules of comedy.

"I love you," Paul said, glancing in the rearview mirror.

"The honor is mine," Tophs replied, a line he'd picked up from *The Greatest Showman*.

Gaps remained in his ability to communicate, and sometimes Tophs's search for a word reminded me of computer coding. In-stead of *train*, he might say, "What is that box thing that moves with those other boxes?"—which sounds like a sentence I'd type into a program with brackets and symbols or describe to Siri in hopes she'd spit out, *Are you looking for train?*

But there were times when he spoke a truth so profound, so sharp, that it almost scared me. On a night we were out to dinner, I asked him to switch seats with me. He cried and screamed for thirty minutes. Paul carried him to the bathroom and then outside until he calmed down. "Tophs, what's wrong?" I asked when he finally came back to the table.

He stared straight ahead over a cooling bowl of pasta. Then, his voice steady: "I'm sad."

"Why are you sad?"

"My feelings make my feelings hurt." In six words, he'd described the greatest struggle of my adult life.

But Tophs's words are often not just about him. He uses them to draw people in and comfort them. While we were living in northern Virginia, Paul's parents moved into an assisted living complex. My father-in-law had gone from a dinner-table theologian and agile racquetball player who stole games from firefighters half his age to a man whose body was imprisoned by Parkinson's. When we visited my in-laws after their move, Tophs jumped out of the van and scurried to my side.

"Mommy, your hand." I gave him my hand, his fingers slim and cold but soft.

"I like holding your hand," I told him.

"Me too. You're the best girl in the world that I have ever seen in my life. I love you."

When his granddad, who could barely speak, opened his mouth and silently wept when he saw us, Tophs was the child who, unafraid, reached out to hug him and held on, putting his head on his granddad's shoulder. "I love you," Tophs told him.

With all his empathy and intuition and wit, maybe I'd made it all up. Or maybe the disconnect was real and had since faded. This is the cycle with Tophs, the ebb and flow of mothering a gift unknown. He's going to be okay, I tell myself; it's just the *how* that I don't know.

Not knowing happens to all mothers, and to all of us, doesn't it? If we are breathing, we are without escape from things we can't know, though I'm not sure to what extent universality softens this blow. Won't we all still look toward days of less pain? Or more knowledge? Or a time when our lack of knowledge isn't so painful?

Sometimes I'm surprised by *what* hurts. The day Tophs's blood sugar dropped to twenty-seven was terrifying, especially once I learned what could have happened. But when I volunteered in his kindergarten classroom and some kid held up a pair of adaptive scissors, saying, "These are Tophs's!" he punched my chest. I replayed that moment all day. *He has small hands. It's no big deal.* But that dent in my chest suggested otherwise: *If he needs special scissors, what else will he need, and how will we know, and what if we don't?*

A slow wearing-down cuts deep too. When, after going months without a potty accident, Tophs started bringing wet clothes home from school, one Ziploc bag at a time, my legs, my will weakened. We could handle wet clothes, I told myself. Who cares? But the random recurrence and our inability to grasp hold of a root cause left me raw and exposed.

The good news is Tophs appears unbothered. But is there grace for the rest of us—the mothers, the families who are still searching? If there's no answer, or no person who can pull us out from the unsolvable space, is that where we will remain?

"We are never more in touch with life than when life is painful, never more in touch with hope than we are then," wrote Frederick Buechner. I don't want these words to be true, exactly. I want the hope to thwart the pain, to ward it off with all its hopefulness. Beneath my sadness, I want every day to be the day when Jesus bursts forth from the tomb in total glory.

But through mothering Tophs, I've come to know a different face of Christ, the one we call the Word. It's the Jesus sitting in the wooden chair, shoulders hunched forward, dark hair hanging over his temples, hiding his face. He may be mourning or pondering, weeping or sighing. He may be turning his world over in his mind with all the purpose and struggle of an infant rolling from her back to her side. He who healed the blind has never let brokenness go unseen. This Jesus. He is the quiet, present one I might have missed had there been no pain. He is the one I look for when I've been emptied of words.

One inviolable rule in our house is Tophs never goes to bed without a snack. A rule reinforced by the memory of that morning when he barely woke up, when his eyes looked glassy and large, when we rushed him to the ER, his body limp and heavy, and walked back through double doors, right into the After.

On a summer evening before we moved from northern Virginia, Tophs slipped out of bed just after I'd tucked him in and asked for another snack. I groaned from my place at the kitchen sink, knowing he'd probably had enough to eat but that I'd never forgive myself *if.* "Get it yourself, Tophs," I snapped. I snapped a lot during those eighteen months, fighting with no one in particular to get back home, to push just one edge of my life out of liminality and over the threshold into familiarity.

He quietly pulled a container of blackberries from the fridge and sat at the kids' wooden table by the kitchen windows. He sat and ate without a word, without even loudly sucking the berries in through his lips as he sometimes did to amuse his sisters. I'm not sure why, but I stopped washing dishes. I pulled out one of those small hard chairs and sat down next to him. He looked at me, lips stained purple, eyes like moons, and then turned his gaze outward, to where the sky slowly swallowed the sun and exhaled thin breaths of peach and rose and plum. And I took him in. I drank deeply while he sat perfectly content as strands of sunlight and shadow made one final stretch across our wooden blinds and onto our hands.

I knew everything about my son in that moment. Everything I needed to know. He watched and ate until the berries were gone, and then he slipped off to bed as quietly as he'd come.

# 23

If you want to try something strange, consider planting a church. Before Paul and I could start our church in Charlottesville, we had to visit Nashville and be assessed by a team of ministers. It was like *The Voice*, except for preachers, and I didn't get to meet Adam Levine. At the end of the week, each couple hoping to plant their own church received a red, yellow, or green light. All I know is we ate a lot of hot chicken, listened to a bunch of sermons, and yada yada yada . . . we got a yellow light. Paul wanted a green. As a perfectionist, I wanted a green too. But, hey, I'd take a yellow. We were finally headed home.

My first morning back in Charlottesville, I awoke relieved. For me, the world always feels most possible in the morning, and even more so in Charlottesville, a place where friends drop off fresh slices of pie and lattes just because. We'd moved in June to a little yellow house on the end of a cul-de-sac, a seven-minute walk from the kids' school. Paul had written a letter to the owners about our family, and before I could joke him about his Mr. Rogers self, they chose our bid over a cash offer. In the fall Eliot would start second grade, and Tophs would start first.

Within a few weeks, Eliot learned to ride a bike, Tophs raced her on his scooter, and I pulled Juliet in a red wooden wagon the school's art teacher gave us for free. This was how life was supposed to be. Things weren't perfect, as the whole world had witnessed the previous summer, but we fit here. I could manage the pace of life.

I sensed, too, that we'd moved further away from Tophs's medical challenges. At his six-year-old checkup, he'd played with handfuls of ponies and looked out the window as Dr. Quillian asked him questions. I'd never felt so far away from the days of triage and investigation, of frantic phone calls and texts. Tophs was Tophs, and it was time to shift our focus. His blood sugar hadn't dropped noticeably for several months; maybe he was outgrowing the condition, just as the shaky red-haired med student had said.

The last time we'd seen Tophs's geneticist, Dr. Humberson, she'd sat on the edge of the examination bed in her white coat and apologized. "We brought you here," she'd said, "and we don't really have more answers for you." The lab had run a free reanalysis of Tophs's DNA sample and found another mutation, also classified as a variant of unknown significance. The only thing I liked about the newest finding was its name. The first three letters were NPR. I considered it a nod to my summer spent interning with host Michel Martin in D.C. I imagined a tiny mutation behind a microphone with a voice like Sylvia Poggioli's.

We were cutting ties, lengthening the distance between us and the doctors. We had no official goodbye, and I still emailed

Shelley with questions now and then, but this shift meant Tophs's case manager at school became one of the most important people in our lives. With his body stable, with us waiting on science and its interpretation, the woman who managed his IEP became the new quarterback. She observed him in class and met with him one-on-one; it wasn't long before we could exchange stories that proved we both understood something about the way Tophs processed material. One of the greatest gifts has been a handful of people who know us and our son, who can talk to us without minimizing the truth that Tophs struggles sometimes. As we transitioned from focusing on Tophs's genes, I began to consider my own again. Now that I'd finished nursing Juliet, I scheduled my first breast MRI.

I drove ten minutes to the medical building and tried to forget the hospice sign I passed on the way in. If I didn't see it, didn't touch it, it didn't exist. There weren't dying people floors above me. No lady in a wheelchair along the side of the building smoking one of her last cigarettes.

Miriam, blonde and petite in black scrubs, led me from the waiting area after I'd changed clothes. I was all too happy to leave behind the woman with glasses who read her book with one continuous frown and the large guy in jean shorts who was the first man to see me in my MRI getup—loose beige pants with an open fly and a pink flowery gown with no bra. I doubt anyone had even noticed, but I prepared a mental apology for someone I might encounter concerned with the location of my boobs: *I swear, they weren't always due south.*

But Miriam had probably imaged a thousand breasts, and she moved easily, sliding my locker key onto her wrist and pointing to a trash can for my gum. Yellow and black signs, warning of radiation or magnetization or scary things I didn't stop to ponder, were plastered on wide wooden doors, and I followed her past a cluster of computers and employees through the door straight ahead.

I tried not to notice. I tried to *do*, not think. If I thought too hard about the thick-walled MRI tunnel, the table sticking out like a tongue, the IV in my right arm, the hard silver bar that would kiss my sternum for the next thirty minutes as I lie facedown, or the hospice above where no one could prevent death, I would regret not taking the Ativan Lindsay had suggested. If anyone should pop an extra antianxiety pill before a medical procedure, it should be me. Yet I've lived with my irrational fear so long, sometimes I think I can control it, charm it quiet like a snake.

My face fit into the cradle, just like on a massage table, she said. I thought of the woman downtown with the soft voice and heavy breathing who kneaded away my tension headaches. This is her table, I told myself.

*Gown is open in the front and breasts hang here, on either side. Scoot up just a bit for me. Good, how does that feel? Arms up by your head.* I didn't know anything about Miriam; in fact, I could no longer see her as she talked to me, but, like Shelley, she was so safe and sure that I almost loved her.

"The machine will get really loud," she warned again. "It sounds like a jackhammer." I can't understand how no one has developed a quieter MRI machine by now. But it wasn't the noise that concerned me as she placed headphones over my ears. It wasn't even getting stuck inside the tunnel. It was the contrast pumping through my veins. My mother had told me she's allergic to it, and what if I was allergic too? Just like we're both

allergic to amoxicillin. Just like we are both BRCA2 positive. It
didn't matter that I'd had an MRI years before with contrast,
no problem. If my throat started to swell or my insides began to
burn, would I be conscious enough to push the call button she'd
placed in my left hand?

Before the test began, Miriam asked what type of music I'd like
to listen to. "Gospel or contemporary Christian," I said. "There's
this guy named Travis Greene."

"You got it."

And then I'm alone, my body moving in and out, to and from
the mouth of the tunnel, and I'm in control of almost nothing.
When the music pipes in, it's as though I'm watching myself on
*Grey's Anatomy*, the camera holding steady for one last shot before
the credits.

It's the artist's same voice, but a song I've never heard. Over
and over again in the chorus, he asks for reasons to trust God.
For an evangelical, his lyrics seem forbidden—God doesn't owe me
any reasons. But my hands are already raised above my head, and
I'm not, half-naked, above begging for more—more reasons, more
God, more answers about this body, this life. I am quiet here, I am
still, in this padded and enclosed church. Miriam is my pastor, the
one who has my ear—*This next part will take three minutes; you're
doing great*—as I go in and out of prayer and sleep and a deep,
deep peace I've rarely known. In the end, I don't want to leave the
sacred space where I've been held and cradled, searched through
and through.

Maybe that's why, a week later, I felt a tricky anger, a sense
of betrayal, when, right before we walked outside for sparklers
on July 4, I got an email. The radiologist had found something

on my scan. It was categorized as probably benign. The report listed the dimensions of the mass, the exact location. Was it like a variant of unknown significance? No one had called me to say, "Hey, there's this thing. It's probably nothing, but we want you to know we're going to follow it. We're not worried."

"What does *probably* benign mean?" Paul asked.

*We need a pumpkin,* Kaitlyn texted.

I was reminded that I could stick my head in the sand, but these differences in our bodies—whether masses or weakened hearts or anxious brains or brains that process more slowly—aren't going anywhere, at least not just because I ignore them. I wonder if you return to a simple truth, but with more knowledge, if that counts as growth.

Days later, I stood in our tiny "master" half bathroom, with the tune of a familiar *less-than* song buzzing between my ears. It's a common way my anxiety manifests as an adult. I'm no longer prone to panic attacks, but I rarely believe I'm good enough or doing enough—as a mother, a writer, a pastor's wife, a friend. I'd gained weight over the last year, I hated my haircut, I was getting old, and I had a mass in my breast that was probably benign. Paul offers one of the best voices of reason against these snowballing thoughts. *You are beautiful. You are sexy. Let's pray. My bride. I married up.*

But Paul wasn't home, and I tend to grow quiet for days before I'm ready to share what I've been processing internally anyhow. Tophs walked in and sat on the edge of my bed in his 4T muscle shirt with painted popsicles and the words I'M COOL LIKE THAT.

"Mommy, you are so beautiful," he said. "It's because of your hair. And I like your shirt and your pants."

I wore a gray church T-shirt and black jeans. "Tophs, you are a gift." I walked over and squeezed my arms around his head and kissed the top. "You are a gift from God."

"Thank you," he whispered, burying his head in my stomach.

24

At age three, Tophs had qualified for special education services under the developmental-delay category, which functioned as a catchall. The label didn't require us to have a cause for delays, just proof they existed. But once a child turns seven, he no longer qualifies for an IEP this way. Paige had seen this day coming and warned me. Paul I were still traveling between cities, hosting meetings in the Charlottesville YMCA and local community centers and serving gigantic slices of our favorite pizza or marzipan-frosted cake, while Paul talked about the kind of church he wanted to build: a church concerned with racial reconciliation, but not at the cost of Black people and our culture. He wanted a unicorn.

I talked to Paige at one of those meetings. "With all of his genetic testing and history of hypoglycemia, you have a case," she said. I put a note in my phone—OHI, or "other health impairment," the category that would probably be a good fit for Tophs in the future. But by the time Tophs turned seven, we'd be back in Charlottesville for good, where people knew us. We'd be back in a small city where individuals mattered.

As we sat around a table at the eligibility meeting held in Tophs's Charlottesville elementary school before his seventh birthday, every educator who'd assessed him said how often Tophs had asked them to repeat instructions or questions during a test. In some academic areas, he scored far above average. Remember his love for LeapFrog videos? He nailed the *Word Attack* portion of the test, scoring above the ninetieth percentile. He hadn't just memorized words like I thought. At some point, he'd learned to decode them. In other areas, he scored in the sixteenth percentile. I found this gap alarming. A representative from central administration, who sat at the head of the table and cut Paul off while just plain ignoring me, said, "Well, sixteenth percentile is average."

*Linda, are you kidding me?*

She Googled ketotic hypoglycemia with us sitting there, in order to prove that Tophs wasn't *routinely* affected by his own body in class. We continued to watch as she championed his strengths in order to deny him.

"When *would* you be concerned?" Paul asked. "What would be considered low?"

"Ohhh, if he were in the twelfth percentile," she said, as though pulling the number from a hat. "I just have trouble seeing where he fits into any of these categories."

I will forever wonder how educators can watch a child struggle and because he doesn't fit exactly into a predetermined box of disability choose to throw him out of the system. When I shared about Tophs's genetic testing and that we didn't know the cause of his hypoglycemia, that there's no name for this Thing, she looked down at her laptop and said, "Okaaaaay. So . . ." and moved right past me.

Maybe you think I raged. But I was done. Drained. For the first time ever in an educational setting, I nearly gave in, accepted defeat, considered turning to outside resources for our child. I sat back in my chair, picked up what had been an iced coffee, and crunched on the leftover ice. Screw it all. I caught eyes with a teacher who had recommended he continue receiving services. She knew how he searched for words and understanding. Her mouth moved just enough, not quite into a smile, to let me know she had to hold it together in the meeting, but this wasn't over.

Another teacher spoke up, frantically, as the meeting wound down. "Where is the data on executive functioning? You can't just send him to second grade. He gets a lot of help throughout the day."

"Well then, we would need more data to show that," the woman from central said.

It was obvious that most of the people who worked closely with Tophs were on our side, his side really. But if Paul had not been sitting next to me, if he had not reversed the inertia by pushing back his chair from the table and saying, "I think we just need a moment to breathe," I would have signed a paper. One that said Tophs was no longer eligible. One that would have decreased the number of Black boys in special education, a goal of the city's that's only whispered behind closed doors. One that would have thrown my boy to the wolves. This exchange, one boy for 1 percent, or one part of 1 percent, one boy for your ledger, one boy for a pat on your back, is criminal.

I remembered the words of another developmental pediatrician who saw Tophs when he was four: *no-man's land*. She wrote: *I worry that school will be hard for him, but because he's not at the very bottom, he'll be expected to do the work of everyone else without the help.*

We pushed back from the table and left.

I pulled into our driveway alone after the meeting, Paul having returned to work. I hadn't tried to fix the achievement gap in ninety minutes or overthrow the school board or secure free breakfast for every child in the nation. I had done something much more possible and impossible: I had tried to make Tophs seen.

I tried and then my chest sank and then I sipped iced coffee. I spoke up and watched my voice evaporate, make not one ripple of difference. I became a person emptied of fire and fight. Then we left. But when we left, Paul was still a professor and pastor, and I was still a mother and writer, but that wasn't fair because Tophs— what options were left for Tophs?

The sound I make is one even I don't recognize. Thin and hoarse, a bruised reed pulled apart. A sound too vacant, too animal, too raw, too *in the beginning*. I am between *from dust* and *to dust,* and I just want him to be okay. I just want him to be okay. I am thinking it, over and over, then I am crying and whispering it to no one behind the pollen-caked windshield of our van.

Later that afternoon, I stood, mostly numb, in my favorite local coffee shop, when Tophs's case manager called. She promised we'd gather more data. She wouldn't give up.

Paul and I wouldn't give up, either. Nothing brings us together quite like a special education meeting. As we left the movie theater one date night, we walked on the downtown mall, past the pizza shop where our kids like to sit in the window, kicking their legs that hang from high stools; past the bookstore that hosts readings for dear, talented friends; past people walking in trios and fours, licking ice cream dribbling down their waffle cones, holding summer off with their tongues. We were an hour past Didion's blue night, alone together. We walked half an inch above the cobblestones that night and didn't feel the dips and drop-offs, the uneven edges. In fact, nothing sharp-edged except the words of the woman who'd dismissed us, who'd started that meeting by questioning whether our son's lack of comprehension was *something else*, something that wouldn't require the state to serve him.

Paul's voice broke through first. "So had you read that before, about accessing the curriculum versus modifying the curriculum?"

After fourteen years of love, of feeling we are too different for a strong marriage in one moment and then not being able to find where our own bodies end in another, I knew he wanted me to override my love for one-word responses and explain. His was a tender invite.

"Yeah, I'll have to read it again, but the article used those phrases to explain the difference between a 504 plan and IEP," I said. This wasn't exactly foreplay. But, then, it was.

Paul had called someone at central office to ask about our case and the district's written policy. "I asked her to give me practical examples of how the two were different," he said, "and she struggled." John Legend could have been crooning on the street corner and it wouldn't have mattered. The passionate tact of Paul made him the most desirable man in the world.

Paul worked his contacts, and I asked Tophs's doctors for letters of support. We read articles on special education law. We wrote notes in the margins of Tophs's assessments and asked others to review them. We contacted a lawyer friend. But mostly, we talked to each other about our boy and about systems, about light and darkness, about inequality and privilege. We spoke a language built by rage and love, sacred, designed just for us, just for this time, just for two kids who fell in love and grew up trying to live right.

# 25

Our family spent most Friday evenings roller skating at a make-shift rink downtown. As soon as Paul walked into the door from work, we grabbed blades, skates, and a helmet for Juliet and drove five minutes to the rec center that opened up its gym for free. Eliot, a natural athlete, took off. Within a few weeks, she was gliding on rollerblades, practicing foot-over-foot turns. Juliet soon refused help, brushing off my arm to venture out on her own Fisher-Price skates. Tophs was focused, always pushing off on the same foot, gliding on the other, his skates like bulky weights around his thin legs. Over the course of several visits, he learned to push off with one foot, then the other, which freed him up to dance. He'd look over at me from behind blue Warby Parker glasses and wave as he rolled by. Soon he was asking me to play "that song from skating" at home on my phone. "Oh, it's called 'Roll Bounce'?" Paul borrowed skates and joined the few brave parents on the floor. I got to sit back and watch, snapping photos and filming. We wrapped up the night with pizza on the downtown mall until we realized that Eliot and Tophs ate pizza for lunch every Friday at school. My Midwest frozen-pizza-loving self was fine with double dipping, but I also ate Ho-Hos growing up, so I let Paul make the responsible decision.

When my sister, nephew, and mom visited for Mother's Day weekend, we took them skating too. My nephew, McClain, is only seven months younger than Tophs but bigger, so Tophs actually wore a hand-me-down Nike tee and a pair of shorts from his cousin that evening. In one photo, Tophs skates, looking down, his arms out and his potty watch, set with alarms, on his left wrist. He skated alone and without much fanfare, reminding me of the older people I've watched swim lap after lap without a splash. In another shot, Paul has given in and allowed Eliot to hold on to the back of his shirt and Tophs to the back of Eliot's, as he leads them around the circle, a kid favorite that usually makes us hold our breath. McClain did not love life on skates, and it was at least an hour past our kids' usual dinnertime, so we left and ordered pizza downtown. We sat inside, and Juliet fulfilled my prophecy that she, the youngest, would eat the most. She ate two whole slices as my sister watched with big eyes and laughed. Tophs didn't quite finish one, but with his cousin around, I chalked it up to excitement. They'd been chasing each other around the house since Eliot and Tophs got home from school and were anticipating dessert next.

We walked up the pedestrian mall to the ice cream shop, where all four kids ordered a multicolored Superman ice cream. Outside they stand in perfect stair steps with cones—Eliot, McClain, Tophs, and Juliet. Eliot and McClain smile straight at the camera. Tophs is bent down, half-smiling, half-looking like he's taking a poo, and Juliet is giving him her standard side eye. When I look closely, I see the unicorn my mom bought him from the toy store in his left hand. Its blue mane and tail turned purple under warm water or against hot pavement. I remember the horn fell out within the first two days, and it looked like someone had shot it through the head.

Paul woke up sometime in the middle of the night and moved to the living room couch with his laptop. Working as a professor while growing a new church meant he rarely slept six hours. He had to preach that Sunday from the stage of the elementary school auditorium where we met, and we'd already committed to a Mother's Day reading at a vineyard on Saturday, where I'd share an essay. We had a lot going on people always said, and they weren't wrong. But when Tophs got out of bed at 3:30 a.m. and seemed wired, like a kid looking for Santa, Paul was there to send him back to bed.

Before dawn, I heard quick footsteps in the hallway. I turned over and saw Paul wasn't in bed.

"Babe?" he called.

"Yeah?" I groaned and turned back over. Why would he make noise so early?

Then he burst through the door. "Where's Tophs's blood sugar thing?"

I jumped out of bed wearing a T-shirt and underwear, grabbed my glasses. I found the diaper bag in the living room and started to pull out the glucometer zipped inside as Paul talked to me with Tophs sitting on his lap.

At 5:00 a.m. Tophs had come out of his room again, this

time his head tilted back and shaking. Drool streamed from his mouth, and Paul rushed him to the bathroom, thinking he needed to vomit. He never did; saliva ran down his chin, his tiny frame tapped, his limbs keeping an awful, ominous beat. Paul saw his son's face drooping on one side. He sat him on the couch and ran to grab apple juice from the fridge.

"Even when I put him down, his leg kept shaking," Paul said.

I listened and froze and fumbled, trying to get the lancets and glucometer out, looking at Tophs, whose neon green WELCOME TO KINDERGARTEN T-shirt was drenched as though he'd been dunked. He looked at me and he looked through me, his mouth on the cusp of a smile. Was he smirking? For a moment, I thought he might be joking. Thought he'd say, "I don't know why I had so much spit in my mouth, Mommy," and run off to bed.

"Should I call?" I asked again, five years since the first time.

"Tophs, when is your birthday?" Paul asked. Tophs had been talking about his seventh birthday nonstop for over a month.

"May twunny-thirrr, twunny-thirrr, twunny-thirrr..."

"Uh, yeah," Paul's eyes locked on mine.

I dropped the glucometer and ran to our room and couldn't find my phone, which was plugged into the wall. "Paul, I need your phone! I need your phone!" Maybe I wasn't built for this. I ran back out, grabbed his phone, and called 911.

I tried to tell the woman on the phone that my son was shaking and drooling and slurring his words, but I was also looking at my son, half himself, half a shell in a T-shirt and striped pajama pants. She had to keep begging for my attention.

"Ma'am? Does he have a fever? Is he breathing? Ma'am?"

By the time the ambulance and fire truck arrived, I'd changed

Tophs into dry pajamas, and he'd grabbed his water bottle, another CamelBak. "Can I bring this with me?" he asked, clearly, holding a toy, as though he hadn't traveled halfway between this life and the next within a span of ten minutes. He wouldn't need the ambulance, but Paul drove him to the ER, where his bloodwork, post–apple juice, didn't show any evidence of hypoglycemia or seizure. The diagnosis on his take-home orders read *altered mental state.*

Tophs was back from the hospital in time to eat breakfast with his sisters and McClain. Somehow the noise hadn't woken my family in the basement, so we told them the story, and I think we all knew, without saying it, what this meant. We had not shut the door, turned the corner. I could no longer pretend that his body, save his mind, had little effect on his day-to-day experiences. I hadn't made, as my parents said when we were kids, "a mountain out of a molehill."

What if Paul hadn't been awake? Where would Tophs had walked? Would he have seized, alone, on the living room floor? The boy who says, "You're beautiful, Mommy. I love the smell of you"—where would he have gone?

I hear the beginning of Mark Nepo's poem "Adrift":

*Everything is beautiful and I am so sad. / This is how the heart makes a duet of / wonder and grief.*

But I tweak the words: *He is so beautiful and I am so sad.*

I could barely connect to the piece I read the next day at the vineyard, the piece that once felt like childbirth, leaving me breathless and excavated as I wrote it. I wanted to tell the kind people who approached me at the table afterward that This Scary Thing Happened to My Boy. Wanted to say how weird it was to stand there, hours later, and read with the rain pouring down outside and bottles of wine being sold inside. I didn't have words for my panic and grief, for the thought that popped into my mind as I'd raced to find my phone and failed: What if this is it? The answer to the moment when I held him and stood on the stairs in the sun and felt the warming urge to cherish him?

But there's another option I've come to consider about that day under the trees. What if I could cherish him *and* not lose him? In my longing and search for a diagnosis, I'd assumed that once we found a name, a label, a house for his symptoms, we'd endure a measure of loss. Maybe not fatal, maybe not the beginning of the end but the beginning of something we'd have to acknowledge and shoulder. A helpful diagnosis for Tophs wouldn't be something as mild as my mitral valve prolapse or as common as a hernia. The relief would come in having a possible path to follow, a community to join with—not necessarily in carrying a lighter load. It's quite possible that living in the liminal space between symptoms and answers has offered me too much loneliness, yes, but also space to breathe, distance from the settled grief of knowing.

# 26

I took Tophs to see Dr. Quillian the following Monday. He'd dyed his hair red along his widow's peak with hair chalk, and he stood on the stool to the exam table and danced, his front tooth missing. He'd recently discovered Kidz Bop and had no idea he was singing the watered-down version of a Cardi B song.

Just a year ago, he'd held ponies with matted manes and stared out the window, and I'd been unsure of how to convey the status of his health. He was "healthy," and he was Tophs. But now, back in familiar territory, I could lead off with fear and danger.

Dr. Quillian tilted her head and listened as I ran through the details of Saturday morning. "On one hand, I don't think we missed the boat in terms of treatment."

I agreed. If there was ever a time she'd lost sleep over Tophs, I hoped those nights were long over, as no one had been able to offer us more than advice on bedtime snacks. And it wasn't negligence or malpractice; it was all they knew.

"I'm just not satisfied . . ." She didn't have to finish. I knew she was talking about the ketotic hypoglycemia diagnosis.

"Sometimes I wonder if you're tired of us," I said. "We've brought you all these questions."

"No! We're in this together."

I believed her.

"I want to help you find out about this awesome boy." She looked at Tophs with his dyed hair, blue-rimmed glasses, and PJs. "We haven't done a full-court press in years to try and crack the code."

This sentence was everything I felt. Also a cliff.

"And I don't know if cracking the code would just be us saying, 'Oh, now that makes sense.'"

Right. An answer doesn't mean a fix. "I'm wondering about the MRI," I said. "Maybe now that he's older, it's time."

She nodded. "I'll consult with Endocrinology and order the MRI," she said. "And I'll revise his letter for school."

We'd asked Dr. Quillian to write a letter of support for our next eligibility meeting. Now she would have to emphasize the unpredictable and dangerous nature of his hypoglycemia, or whatever might have caused the seizure. In my daydream, Paul and I walk into the next meeting, throw the letters on the table, and say, "Not much to report except that *he had a seizure.*"


"I remember I had a lot of drool in my mouth," Tophs said about the episode. When he came home from the ER, he told us the doctor *cut* his arm to get the blood out.

"Oh, they drew blood to make sure you were healthy?"

"Yeah, yeah, Mommy. It hurt a little."

I've told him the reason we feed him before bed is to keep him from getting sick. "I need protein?" he asks. "Yes, protein is good for you, and also some carbohydrates." I'm never sure how to describe a carb (I took zero science classes in college), and I don't dwell on the fact that sometimes even a snack full of fat and carbs or protein isn't enough. I don't tell him that maybe what we know isn't quite enough. Perhaps all the running around with his cousin and siblings that Friday had triggered it. And he hadn't eaten a snack after school—just a Jolly Rancher he'd earned as a prize from his teacher. Then we'd had a late dinner after skating, and even though I'd thought ice cream around eight could replace the regular snack, maybe I'd been wrong. Or, as the one endocrinologist suggested, maybe we'd staved off several hypoglycemic episodes with snacks over the last five years but, of course, didn't have the proof. I'd like to think that's true. That we'd been *doing* something.

On the school front, Paul and I got what Tophs needed. We walked into the next eligibility meeting and didn't have to say a word. The woman in charge of this "team" effort did not make eye contact or offer an apology, but she completely changed her tune. I didn't feel like she'd heard us, just that something had been handed down from up the ladder. That would suffice for now.

But before we left, we shared that if *this* was how these meetings were generally conducted, we were concerned for other kids who might have one parent trying to manage everything or a sibling with disabilities. What about kids who don't have a dad with a career in education? There are so many ways I could see children of color and children from low-income families left to drown.

Someone in the room needed to learn that you shouldn't need white skin or a PhD or lots of money to be heard. And if race and class aren't the issues, if the issue is that a student must have a crystal-clear diagnosis, then say so. Until then, I will believe the whispers I heard: the city needed fewer Black boys in special education, and my Black boy almost got caught up in the quota. Maybe it wasn't an intentional scheme, surely it wasn't a written policy, but it could derail lives of the most vulnerable nonetheless.

I'm not sure at what age Tophs will recognize that he needs support. Maybe he already does. I suppose we'll handle it similarly to how we've talked to Eliot, who is completely secure telling her friends she sees a "feelings doctor." Tophs might see a "processing doctor." After having Juliet, I've realized the lack of complex or lengthy conversations I've had with Tophs originates from those critical years when, as a preschooler, he couldn't engage in much back-and-forth. I learned to speak slowly, to give one-step directions and wait. I learned to use visuals and give him time to slip into his imaginary world of figurines and ponies.

When Juliet began asking questions as a toddler, it hit me in real time, rather than through videos: I didn't have these moments with Tophs. I still talk more slowly and clearly to my kids, which isn't a bad habit by any stretch, but it's been molded mostly by Tophs's needs, and also by Eliot's, who occasionally stutters. As a preschooler, Juliet understood when the nurse gave her a flu shot— where the needle went in and how it felt. She talked to me about the process afterward. When I took Tophs to the doctor at that age, I just held him tight and searched his eyes; Dr. Quillian even leaned in and kissed his forehead as the nurse drew blood once, but he didn't budge or react, and I didn't know what to say, except,

"All done! Good job!" There has been a gap, and we're still filling some of it in with words.

As Paul drove us to the gym one Saturday, Tophs started a conversation between his doll and Juliet's.

"Can I tell you something Martin Luther King said?" Tophs's doll asked. "Say yes," he whispered to Juliet.

"Yes," Juliet's doll answered.

"One day in Alabama, little Black boys and Black girls and white boys and white girls will join hands as brothers and sisters. It's true! It's really true!"

I smiled at Paul. *Did you hear that?* Now I was the only one whispering.


Gone were the days when I didn't have to explain medical procedures to Tophs. As I prepped him for his brain MRI, which we would attempt without sedation, I stayed vague about the why. *You know how you got sick before your birthday? This machine will take a picture of your head. We just want to make sure it looks really good.* I avoided the word *bruin*, though I'm pretty sure he'd read it in a booklet the child life specialist emailed me. I worried if I shared too much, he'd fixate on something being wrong with his brain. Even though he's not me, maybe he'd obsess over death and destruction, danger rather than safety.

We discussed the tunnel, how it would be open on each side, how he wouldn't be locked in but should be very still. I hoped he'd choose the DVD option; they offered to use a mirror and screen so that he could watch a movie during the test. Instead, he opted for Kidz Bop. Seeing as he had a whole routine with staccato air punches for their version of Cardi B's "I Like It," I had a hard time believing music would be the best choice.

Shelley's word had always been gold. She and Dr. Humberson erred on the side of avoiding an MRI unless Tophs met one of three criteria. His head circumference was close to the fiftieth percentile but not quite over the mark. He had never regressed; he didn't learn to walk and then stop. And, up until two weeks before his seventh birthday, he'd never had a seizure. No one would actually say Tophs had a seizure. It was hard to know. But everyone agreed whatever it was, it was scary. Never wanting to be accused of inaccuracy, I would say "seizure-like episode." I told two girlfriends, both moms and married to doctors, about Tophs's episode over dinner downtown one night. We sat outside on the patio and ordered drinks and small plates as people strolled the mall. My friends didn't even pause when I finished. "Um, Taylor, that's a seizure," they both said. "Like, that's what a seizure is." *Okay, okay. Pass the bread.*


Paul and I stuffed Tophs's clothes, vibrating potty watch, and glasses into a hospital locker, and changed him into loose hospital pajamas. Subjecting your kid to a procedure that isn't an emergency and might not yield anything requires a certain distance. I had no idea if Tophs would panic once inside. What did panic look like on Tophs? Would it scar him?

The contraption the tech placed around his head didn't exactly comfort me. Think 1980s orthodontal headgear. He lay on a table, hands at his sides, and they placed his head inside a helmet, which also had a mirror at the top. Even as he listened to music, he could look into the mirror and see us sitting a few yards from his feet. I stared at my son's dark eyes, saw the rise of his cheekbones. The dancer, the jumper, the funny-face maker. He doesn't change just because we are looking at his brain. Tophs is Tophs.

"Okay, Christopher, just try to hold real still for us." Tophs straightened up. But a minute later, he pulled his little knees up under the white sheet. God, I hoped this wasn't the cover of Ariana Grande's "7 Rings." We would lose him altogether.

In another moment, he seemed to forget where he was and started to sit up, as though he could reach us. I didn't want to smile and make him laugh and shake his shoulders or bring his hand to his mouth. But I didn't want to appear concerned either. *We are with you, Tophs. I don't even know if this is fair, but here we are.*

After forty minutes, the tech announced he was done. Tophs came down from the table, asking about the music. "I didn't know a lot of the songs. Was it Kidz Bop?"

Beginning that afternoon, and for several weeks after, Tophs had accidents. He'd be riding in the van or playing at home and a shadow would grow across his pants. We'd seen a high tide of accidents before but never found a cause or correlation. It was hard not to wonder if he'd been scared inside that tunnel, even though he only spoke of the music and the Sprite he picked out from the hospital's mini fridge. Tophs, who returned home to Eliot's questions: Did it hurt? Were you scared? *It was okay.* Tophs, the unbothered hero of it all.

I'm not sure it's healthy to straddle this fence, but on one side I belong to the land of "Tophs is just Tophs," where we assume, for sanity's sake, that we will never know the source of illness or challenges. We say things like, "Maybe, one day, some scientist in

Europe will find the root . . . but we'll be okay if not, because he is so wonderful, more than a treasure."

On the other side, the clock keeps ticking. New pathways are being created and there are specialists he has yet to see. There is more to be done, because if we won't do it *now* for our child, then when?

Soon after his MRI appointment, we drove as a family to a clinic at Children's Hospital of Philadelphia. When I had mentioned the possibility to Dr. Quillian, for the first time ever, she said, "You know what? If he were my child, I would take him. If it's in-network and you have the time, you've got nothing to lose."

Several doctors had recommended the clinic to us, and the visit was in-network, so we only paid for the hotel. For a week before we left, I pricked his finger every morning before breakfast and recorded his blood glucose level. For his trouble, Tophs received a pinch of Nerds in his palm.

CHOP is an immaculate high-tech palace, everything designed with kids in mind. I rolled a laptop around with me to complete our registration, and the doctor who saw Tophs looked over his records and test results on a large TV screen in the exam room as he talked to us. I wish I could say we learned something new. I mean, we did. We learned a lot about what can go wrong with the endocrine system and insulin levels; we learned that kids with ketotic hypoglycemia generally look like Tophs—short and slim; we learned that even specialists like this doctor aren't sure why these kids can't fast like most kids, even toddlers, can.

The doctor went into far more detail than any other endocrinologist had. Yet, even as he explained the way our livers store glycogen, I couldn't help but think of Tophs's elevated AST level, though I knew it was only slightly high and is not necessarily tied to his liver function. As the doctor discussed glycogen storage diseases, it seemed clear Tophs didn't have one, and yet I thought about the one mutation that renders him a carrier of the disease. He should be symptom free. Only his future children should be at risk, depending on the genes of his mate, but that's just what we know. I'm not sure I'll ever believe in the true coincidence that a kid who carries this genetic mutation just happens to experience dangerously low levels of glucose. How could a slice of pizza and scoop of ice cream, a combination the doctor said should be perfect, leave Tophs shaking and slurring several hours later? The doctor didn't know, but his last words to us were, "I think he'll be okay."

In the car, I stayed silent, my mind reeling. I'd wasted time and money, disrupted the kids' schedule. Friends had been praying about this appointment. I'd let them down. With the automatic negative thoughts closing in, I wanted to break away. I tried to breathe, then turned to Paul.

"What did you think?"

He was navigating the city traffic, knowing we'd have fifteen potty stops ahead of us. "I thought it was encouraging," he said. That was it. That was Paul's world. I wish I could reach in and steal some of that.

"I feel like I wasted your time, everyone's time, I don't know..."

"I think we took him to the best, and he said he thinks Tophs'll be okay. So now we don't have to wonder if we should have gone."

End of story. His words, his thoughts, didn't reconfigure mine, exactly, but they gracefully gave me pause, kept me from falling face first into doubt.

## 27

This time I didn't drop a dollar bag of July 4 pop-its onto the kitchen floor in panic when the email came. This time, the results belonged to Tophs.

IMPRESSION: *No evidence of intracranial abnormality.*

Not probably, not likely, not a variant of uncertain significance.

The relief from reading Tophs's MRI results came slowly before it roared through my chest: I did not ruin him. I am not a mother who breaks things. My relationship with my boy, my love for him, is not, as one of his test results has read, likely pathogenic. My role as a mother has been shadowed in shame, tested by the limits of science, dissected through the lens of faith. But, overall, it has been benign. Not perfect, full of familial quirks and missteps, but positively benign.

Day by day, shame sloughed off. Relief is the afterlife of something undesired. You are stressed and then not, in pain and then
not, you are concerned and then not. I thought relief was a suddenly word, not a word that could smolder or spread. A week out,
two weeks, then a month, then three months, and I would catch
myself walking into the gym or under balding trees, remembering,
and suddenly (*here* is the suddenness) breathing in deeply, my lungs
storing more air than before, as though new alveoli had formed. I
did not break him. What's more, he's not broken.

To be sure, I believe pieces within all of us are broken or
lacking or heading south, facing decay. Whatever caused Tophs's
carnitine to plummet, whatever caused ketotic hypoglycemia—*if*
that's what he has—cannot be declared healthy or optimal. The
seizure that made his hands and legs tap at dawn is not what I
would choose for my son. These conditions may be treatable. The
difficulty he has comprehending text can be improved. But that is
not the same as: no evidence of abnormality. I'm not sure how to
square all of this, to hold both or *all* truths in tension, to make
meaning and order from the chaos of hope and disappointment, of
prayer and reality.

Maybe I can start with myself: I am a witty artist with a lot of
laughs and love to give, who hates being vulnerable in person and
has contemplated ending her life. Tell me, then, what to make of
the anxiety and depression that have plagued me. Do not call me
strong. Do not create a cheap scale with the dark moods on one
side and the comedy on the other.

What of the BRCA mutation and the two ovaries and the two
breasts that fed my children, that gave them a fine start? I'm looking for what's whole and holy in our bodies and minds that has

nothing to do with a perfect test result. I'm looking for the ways bodies created from dust can hold glory.

In the Church, Jesus is often a haloed baby or crucified body; he is a fish multiplier or water strider. What if we talked about the time Jesus shook with fever? Maybe he never got the flu, maybe he cut his hand collecting wood or woke up with brain fog after the death of his dear friend Lazarus. What if we had more imagination for the incarnate part of God incarnate? What if I have lazily cordoned off as mystery parts of my faith that were always intended to be explored? What if unknowable does not mean unsearchable?

I look at photos from Tophs's first day of life: Paul's thumb wrapped around a striped hospital beanie, my son's cleft chin, the long lines casting down diagonally from the inner crevice of each eye to his cheeks. *Who are you, buddy? Tell me. Mommy needs to know. Is it all wrapped inside of you right now? Tell me what is an expression of those cells, something I can't change, and tell me if you're okay or if it's hard for you. Show me how shapes fit together for you, how movies delight you, how you remember Maya Angelou's birthday after she's gone.*

All of this. Every test. Every observation. Every appointment. Every single meeting. Every finger and toe prick. Every video of head-banging and stimming saved as evidence. *It's all just me, your mommy, standing still as the tide recedes, waters drawing sand too quickly from under my feet. It's me calling over my shoulder to ask if you're okay. This is all I really need to know, Tophs.*

My own mother, holding my head in a hospital beanie, could not have known what lay hidden in my genes—what made me anxious, kept my brain leaking light, sent my heart galloping. Couldn't have known the risk for breast cancer within a breastless baby girl. I wonder if she looked at me and asked, "Just who are you, Taylor? Mommy needs to know."

Mom, if you're reading this: It is hard, and I am okay. It is both.

I cannot pretend to understand how we are formed by God, seen and known in the Before, then born in fragile, resilient bodies that hurtle toward growth and decay. Yet we are seen and not abandoned. My God, this is hard.

As he's gotten older, Tophs has asked deeper theological questions. The kind that seem a mismatch for his age. "When we die and Jesus blesses us and we get back alive, will we still be Black?" He and Paul were simply sitting on the couch, no Bible in sight.

"You know, that's a good question, Tophs, and I don't know for sure." Paul, forever calm and encouraging.

"When we die and Jesus blesses us and we get back alive, will we be babies or will we be like the age we were?" How had I never even come near this thought? As soon as he asked, I couldn't unthink it.

On a Sunday morning in the fall, several months into our church plant, after we'd grown from catered meetings in our living room to gatherings at the local Boys and Girls Club, black fans cooling us in the heat, to one larger service in a school auditorium, Paul spoke about baptism. Our church would hold its first round of baptisms at the rec center's indoor pool next door. I sat with our kids in chairs that clapped together when we stood, drinking coffee, praying for a miracle—that no more plastic water bottles would drop from my children's hands to the sloped floor, rolling all the way down to Paul's feet in front of the stage. I thought Tophs was there because he had to be, as a pastor's kid.

"I think I wanna get baptized," Tophs said after church.

"Do you know what that means, Tophs?" Paul asked.

"I think it means you love Jesus? Yeah, I wanna go in the water."

"I'm scared to get baptized," Eliot shared. She'd started taking communion the year before when Paul explained the meaning of the wafer and grape juice. She believed in Jesus but would be better off getting sprinkled with water on her forehead. I get it, Elie. The idea of someone, even someone you love, holding you under.

"I'm not scared. I wanna do it. Can I, Daddy? Can I get baptized?"

Paul talked to Tophs again to ensure this wasn't just his latest obsession, like going to Target to buy an L.O.L. doll. "I think he gets it," he said.

*It goes in his mind.*

I am the parent checking blood sugar at night, taking one good look at our son sleeping before I go to bed. I am the parent who knows how much sugar and protein he should eat and exactly where the mutations are in his genes, but Paul is the parent who can safely draw Tophs into the water, without even trying.

In a favorite picture, Paul, dressed in a gray suit and satin tie, prepares to read a scripture at my sister Autumn's wedding. He's holding a page out in front of him, sitting on a wooden pew in that Catholic church where I sat in Umbros. And on his lap, leans, not really sits, baby Tophs, not yet four months old, Paul's left hand supporting his son's neck and head, the top of his back. Between Paul's chin and Tophs's lips, on a diagonal, rests a bottle, leaking milk into Tophs's mouth. Father works and feeds, gives of himself, gives to his boy, won't let his son slip or go hungry. I can't think of anything more Paul.

On our church's first baptism Sunday, Tophs sits poolside with a small group of kids and adults, wearing a black Victory Church T-shirt and red trunks. Even on this stage, he smiles and makes silly faces, seemingly at home with his place on the silver bleacher, in the water, in the world. When Paul calls his name and walks over to the shallow end, Tophs jumps down the stairs, holding on to each metal bannister as he goes, bopping his head as though they're playing his walkup song. At the bottom, he pushes up on the railings with both arms like a gymnast and kicks his feet with a grin.

Paul grabs him under his arms and pulls him in deeper. Before he can even begin his brief talk, Tophs plugs his nose and starts humming a song he's made up.

"Tophs, upon confession of your faith—"

"Do-deh-do-do-do . . ."

He's saying something I can't quite make out as Paul prepares to lower him down. It sounds like, "Are we gonna do this?!"

"I now baptize you in the name of the Father, the Son, and the Holy Spirit." Tophs takes one big breath, still pinching his nose, and as Paul guides him back and under, his feet flutter kick, breaking the surface once more. Before there's time to panic, to half imagine him swallowing too much water, there's his head, glistening and wet, Paul's hand on the front of his son's chest, holding a boy who has hit a home run, stolen a base. The crowd cheers and claps for the boy who is all angles and bones, his skinny brown limbs most round and full in the arms of his father.

Tophs climbs out of the pool, and I wrap him in the heavy beach towel Autumn gifted him for Christmas. "That was fun! I wanna get baptized again!"

*Enjoy him. Hold him. Stay right here.*

# 28

Tophs, eight, crawled into my bed one morning and hugged me. "You'll always be a great mommy," he whispered.

A week before, I'd dreamed he was in the bathtub. I walked away to check something on my computer or call my mom, something that could have waited. I knew I had to hurry, could feel the need to rush. *You never leave a child alone in the bath*, said a small voice in my subconscious, *even one his age*. When I stepped back into the bathroom, his head was halfway underwater, his tongue sticking out through a layer of bubbles. He didn't look well, like he'd taken in water. I pulled him out and stood him up, noticing how red his back had turned.

"I think something happened." But he couldn't tell me what.

I am left to wonder. In dreams, in life. In life about the dreams I've had and whether they are meaningless. Eliot is wondering too.

In the bathtub with her siblings one morning, she recalled a dream about Tophs in water:

"I had a dream that Tophs ran and jumped into the bath. He wanted to have fun, and he didn't see how high the water was, like up to the ceiling, and he couldn't get out. Daddy was cutting his hair or something and didn't notice, and Mommy said, 'Babe! Don't you see him?' And Daddy lifted him up."

I did not ask what happened next. Are these dreams summaries or prophecies, strange side effects, even, of living during a pandemic?

After school abruptly ended in March, COVID-19 cases rising across the U.S. and world, Tophs didn't seem too bothered by the change. He liked his school-issued laptop and hadn't started to miss traveling beyond our cul-de-sac. But soon the CDC suggested masks, and we warned Tophs he should not jump from one couch arm to another over hardwood floors because we didn't want to visit the ER, especially not *now*.

"Mommy, if that drooling thing happens to me again, what will we do? Will we still go to the hospital?"

He'd had a second seizure that winter, right before Christmas, much like the first, with slurring and drooling. I'd grabbed a blood glucose reading while Paul, panicked, tried to spoon peach juice into his boy's unswallowing mouth. As the stupid hand ticked on the glucometer's screen, I just knew it had to be dangerously low. Maybe thirty, even less.

Two-ninety-seven. His blood sugar was *high*. The ambulance arrived and took him this time, along with Paul, to the hospital.

What could high blood sugar mean? This had to be the key. But the chief endocrinologist, paged by the ER physicians, didn't want to be bothered, Paul said. He walked in and asked, "What can I do for you?" as though we needed a new sandwich or windshield wiper. To the high reading, he said, "As long as the number goes back down, we don't worry too much."

Other doctors were more curious than that endocrinologist, and Tophs did undergo an EEG of his brain. The results were slightly abnormal yet not diagnostic. The neurologist still hesitated to use the term *seizure*. "I don't want to rush to put him on seizure medication if that's not what this is," she said.

"A lot of things are wrong with me, and a lot of things happened to me," Tophs said after his EEG, sitting and playing on the floor.

I crouched down next to him. "What do you mean?"

"Like I think when a lot of drool came out of my mouth."

"There are also a lot of amazing things about you that I've never seen in anyone else," I said. As though I hadn't been thinking about this for six years. As though any parent could be prepared for this moment after six years. "I love you very much."

I shopped for groceries, masked and alone, returning home to wipe down cardboard boxes of frozen waffles and paper packets of taco seasoning. Tophs asked the same question a few times, and I tried to reassure him. We'd visited the Cleveland Clinic the week before the U.S. shut down, the two of us flying to Ohio and eating thin-crust pizza with my family in Bexley the night before his visit, perfectly ignorant of what was to come that spring. A wonderful nurse practitioner and a nutritionist at Cleveland's pediatric glycogen storage disease clinic had helped us alter his diet to include more protein and less sugar. They saw other kids, like Tophs, who were genetic carriers of the disease but also showed dangerous symptoms. Since the visit, I'd been checking his glucose every night and could normally guess the number within several points. We'd reached a place that was well-boundaried, if not completely normal or safe.

"You know how you've been eating five grams of sugar? And more protein? I think that's really helping. I don't think you'll have another episode anytime soon, but if you did, we could still take you to the hospital."

"Okay." He didn't fight me. *He's just a little anxious*, I thought. *He's processing. He's growing up. This is good.*


The night after Tophs hugged me in bed, he woke up from a bad dream and found Paul, who was already up working at 3:30 a.m. "I had an accident," he said, and Paul washed him in the hallway bathroom, even though his pajamas didn't feel wet, and let him lie down next to me in bed. *How sweet*, I thought, and fell back asleep.

The sound of his retching, the feel of his polite patting, as though he felt guilty asking for help, woke me. I opened my eyes to Tophs standing on my side of the bed, vomiting nothing, a strand of drool running down his chin, the lonely marker of a body gone wrong. I jumped up and patted his back, even though I knew he wasn't vomiting, not choking. What do you call the thing you do, knowing it's fruitless?

"Baaaaaabe?!" I made the unsettling call to Paul, code for, "Can you help, can anyone help?"

Paul ran in and flipped on our bedroom lights. Had Tophs's eyes been closed the whole time, or just now from the brightness? "Tophs, can you open your eyes? Can you open your eyes?" It took a few moments, but he did. Then Paul walked toward our door. "No!" was all I could scream, but he didn't listen. He left.

I guided Tophs's body to sit on the bed. He was sitting, not shaking, maybe he was fine. As I reached for the glucometer on my nightstand, our best shot at solving this case, Paul walked back in, holding his phone as a weapon—or maybe a tool—the way we've seen people on TV record the police.

On the video, you see Paul's feet rushing over hardwood floors and then Tophs's lashes and fuzzy mohawk. It's 4:46 a.m. when Paul, the same man I met on the trolley, reaches his hand to his son, and gently asks, "Tophies?" and Tophs looks up, his right eye half-shut, his lips and chin painted with saliva. "Hey, buddy, can you tell me your birthday?"

Tophs smiles, his mouth only rising on one side, as though he's smirking, as though *this question is so silly, Daddy.*

"May thumy," he whispers, voice like gravel. A bubble forms over his lips. He smiles more.

"Okay," Paul whispers back, a tender call and response.

"Yeseee," Tophs mumbles.

"Okay," he strokes the back of his son's head. *Well done.*

In the background, the *zip* of the glucometer pouch.

"Can you tell me again?" Paul asks, cupping Tophs's head.

"May . . . May-twuhn . . ." He looks toward me and grins, as though I should make this guy stop acting funny. "May . . ." and blinks his eyes. So sweet, even as his body betrays him.

"Okay, okay," Paul says. "Okay, bud."

"Good job, buddy," I say, pricking his finger.

A little bubble comes and goes on his bottom lip as he breathes and looks down. The video cuts, but I know the rest by heart:

Eighty-five. It's eighty-five. His blood sugar is normal?

I check it again. Ninety.

We gather his urine in a sample cup just in case and let him sip Gatorade Zero from a plastic church cup, because what do you do for a child whose blood sugar hasn't crashed after all? Instead of calling an ambulance, I text Shelley at this absurd hour to tell her this absurd thing: another seizure, normal glucose.

Shelley, along with a kind and thorough geneticist new to UVA who had recently taken over Tophs's case, called me that morning.

"So with the normal blood sugar reading, it makes me think what's going on in his body isn't just metabolic," the doctor said. "I think we should consult with Neurology again."

It wasn't so much what she said but the way I could almost hear her mind spinning, cataloguing everything she'd learned about genetics during her time at the NIH, thinking back to Tophs's records, which she'd studied in detail, wondering if there was any way she could be wrong in her conclusion. In our last appointment, we'd discussed the possibility that Tophs had a disorder of gluconeogenesis, or a problem making glucose. A seizure with normal glucose changed everything.

Three days later, a masked Tophs completed a forty-minute EEG on his back, in the cold basement of the hospital, during which a well-meaning but old-school tech threatened to turn off the cartoons if he kept squirming. "You're doing great, buddy," I told him, loud enough for her to hear.

Of course, the results came at night, online, with words like *delta waves* that meant nothing to me. At the bottom of the report, in a summary by the doctors who read the lines and sparks of his brain: *EEG abnormal.* But the first had been abnormal too. Just nonspecific, and on the heels of a normal MRI, the neurologist had advised us to control his blood sugar as best we could and to watch and wait.

Watch and wait and test. Rarely treat. The silver-lining gnome living rent-free in my head said, "Be thankful. You don't have to treat him. It's not serious enough to require daily medication. Rejoice!"

But watch, wait, and test—rarely treat—has proved its own burden, its own prescription without end. The eternal nature of a position, no matter how good or bad, has always haunted me. On the bad side, it's the pain of labor. All three times I went into labor, I worried the pain would never end. And on the good side, it's heaven. Even as someone who believes I'll spend forever with Jesus, a God I love a whole lot, I'm beside myself some nights trying to quantify eternity. I wake up in a sweat, my mind trying to grasp hold of a thing without end. I'm not sure if treatment would be a welcome interruption or an eternity all its own.

Tophs sat next to me on our basement futon for the tele-health visit with the neurologist. "Is it okay for him to be here?" I asked.

"Yes, I actually have a couple of questions for him, and then it's up to you, but he can stay." She wanted to know what he remembered about the last *episode*, as we still called it.

"I woke up, and I think I had a lot of drool in my mouth, yeah, and my dad was too far away this time, I think, so I saw my mom and she was closer, and I think I like tapped her?"

I've had no training for what came next, so as the conversation turned to results and her concern, I turned to Tophs. "Go upstairs, bud. You're all done."

"Awww, I kinda want to stay," he whined.

"Nope, go play. I'll be right up."

The neurologist described the activity on his EEG: all kinds of sparks, on both sides of the brain, in the front and the back. Too many, I gathered, to sit and watch.

"How's his learning?" she asked.

How to describe Tophs's educational and developmental record in a sentence or two?

"What I saw from his EEG—if that's happening during the day, it could mean that his brain *sparks*, for lack of a better word, and then goes blank."

I knew she understood long and short brain waves and all the other jargon, but I appreciated her mundane term. I wouldn't forget *sparks*. The idea of a short circuit during a math or reading lesson. That made sense.

She also used the previously forbidden word. "I think we can call them seizures now with this latest EEG and the fact he's had three that were so similar. They still seem a little strange, but they're so consistent."

The new geneticist's words echoed in my head: "I once had a patient in residency who ate ice cream during her seizures."

"The other thing that concerns me is that these seizures happen at night, in his sleep."

"Right." She didn't have to finish. I wasn't crazy to check on him every night.

"But take your time deciding about medication. I don't want to rush you, but I think with these latest results, it's appropriate to consider."

Some decisions take a lot of prayer and research, but others? Maybe others you just make. We wouldn't know for over a year if the medication helped, because, as scary as they were, Tophs's seizures happened every six to seven months. I'd measure out a clear liquid, twice a day, for twelve to eighteen months, unless anything changed.

*My son needs seizure medication.* Can a psalm be an objective fact? This time, the neurologist hadn't used the word *epilepsy.* Why hadn't I asked if he had epilepsy?

In the days after the appointment, I revisited dark waters, grief clinging thick. Meanwhile, in the midst of more unknown in 2020 than I could handle, more than our nation and the world could handle, Tophs rocked back and forth on an exercise ball, easily navigating between tabs on his laptop. This time he tapped away for virtual school, not one-click Amazon shopping, typing answers to prompts from his teacher. He swiped his finger between screens to show me.

The first prompt read: I am _____. On a bright virtual post-it note, my boy had typed: *perfectly made.*

*A lot of things have happened to me and I am perfectly made.* Tophs's psalm. My boy's gentle offering to us all.

# 29

And in enduring mystery, we need just enough
light to take one more step.
—Tish Harrison Warren,
*Prayer in the Night*

After I've done all I can, after I've felt his forehead at night for clamminess and turned up the baby monitor in case he seizes; after I've taught him to check his own blood sugar and call out the number to me; after I've read *Bad Kitty* books with him on the couch, checking his fluency and comprehension; if the fear or guilt still overwhelms, I can lean into Paul.

In the last year, I've come back to that young woman sitting in the booth at Ruby Tuesday. The one who allowed an effusive, dizzying love to overtake her fear of shame, long enough to confess, "I just don't want to be falling by myself." Sure, he was leaving her roses, baking her cinnamon swirl cakes, but, still, she took a chance.

Back then, it was falling in love; now, the falling is in love, in parenting, in fear. And in grief. It's so much weightier, but the vulnerability, the standing naked as in the beginning, that is the same. It's Paul's hand I need when the worst, the thing beyond what I feared, seems to be happening.

It took me four years to schedule the surgery. Coming from the operating room, I am one of Dalí's pocket watches, flung over a branch and melting, sliding toward whatever awaits below.

"Taylor. Taylor. How do you feel?" The voices are behind and over me.

A Mack truck has smashed into my chest, left shards of hot metal to burn under the front of my gown. What a strange trick they help you play on yourself—to fall asleep under a heavy gas mask and neon light, only to awaken and remember *something happened*. They did something. You asked them to. There's one slice of one moment before you remember the reason you are here, burning.

My breasts are gone.

My body, made of nausea, has turned on me, and I will vomit my entire self up and out through my mouth. They are pushing me, rolling me through space, a cold cloth on my forehead to fight the sweat that has drenched me. Careful, or I'll slide down the right side of the bed onto the floor. The world is two dimensions, and my voice has been replaced by a thin pocket of air.

"Sick," I push the word out. I have to show them I am alive, even though I want to die. My fight-or-flight response has also come to, and if *this* is how living feels after surgery, I want out.

As quickly as I've moved from sleep to wakefulness, my nausea dissipates, the walls right themselves, and I'm more myself. I had to take out my contacts, so I can't see well, but my nurse is a Black woman with a mask and glasses and short natural hair. She's blurry, and Black people don't age anyhow, so she could be anywhere from twenty-nine to seventy-two. Anika always stands to my left, except when she calls Paul on the room's phone.

"Can you have him bring me a Mr. Pibb?" I ask, high off normalcy. I don't yet know my blood pressure dropped at the end of surgery. Don't know that what I experienced was not the normal side effects of anesthesia but what a doctor friend called "a brief period of shock."

I am fine, everything is fine, Paul will bring a Pibb. Does he know Wegman's sells twelve-packs, and Bodo's has it on fountain? Paul doesn't drink much soda, or any coffee. America might run on Dunkin', but Paul runs on water. My least favorite of any soda is the bottled twenty-ounce kind, but I'd even take that. He'll figure it out. He always does, always has, even back when we were barely dating.

"I have something for you," he said, handing me a bottle on one of his trips to Charlottesville my third year. I'd looked at the fat white pill bottle with a red lid, the original label replaced with one of his own making: I.F. Pills (Take as needed).

I could only laugh. *I.F.* stood for *intimate friendship*, a term we'd probably read in a Joshua Harris book. It described this strange space of getting to know each other, of crushing really hard, of going on dates but not dating. It's not a practice I would ever push on another couple now, but I also don't regret what Paul and I cultivated. I mean, the guy was emptying Tylenol bottles to show his love. He'd stuffed cotton balls in the bottom and several strips of paper "pills." They read *a home-cooked meal* and *a foot massage* and *Humpback Rock*, which, despite how it sounds, was not code for sex. *A visit to Ohio* read one, and I stopped.

"Are you serious? You would drive me to Ohio?"

"Just say when."

Paul had this way of making spectacular or far-off ideas seem possible. Why would he drive me seven hours to Ohio? But if he said it, he'd make it happen.

I don't know the exact moment when people in scrubs started looking at me and making calls to other floors of the hospital. Anika, over my left shoulder, looking at the monitors. Talking to someone behind her. "She's tachy."

I know that word. It's not unusual for my pulse to run high. I'm flat on my back still; they haven't raised my head and chest because of the low blood pressure. I hear my heartbeat thrumming in my ears. Loud, strong, a drumline of my own. I don't worry.

Until a doctor peeks in through the curtain and talks aloud to others. "It's too early for *that*," he says. A medical board meeting is happening at my feet. "Let's get a chest X-ray."

Within minutes, someone slides a dark slab under me. When they leave, I turn to Anika. Maybe if I say it, that will help. "I'm scared."

"Oh, no, dear. What are you scared of? There's nothing to be scared of. You're gonna be just fine." She grabs my hand in her blue glove, lets me dig my nails in.

I want to believe her. I don't.

The doctor who ordered the X-ray returns, pushes a button on a machine to my right. He pulls the long receipt from the printer, holds it up in the dusk of my room. "Whoa, that's a long QT." He turns to his friend in white and says a number that starts with five.

How many times had I read about long QT syndrome in high school?

"Yeah, when this happens in the ICU . . ." the friend in white starts, and then the voice fades, leaving me aflame in fear.

"Let's call up to Cardiology."

I squeeze Anika. *This is it. I am not safe.* I thought Tophs's test had revealed the BRCA mutation, but it's revealed a defect in my heart, something I'd long suspected. I search her covered face as best I can. "What's wrong with me?"

"You are gonna be fine, Taylor. They're just running some tests. I'm right here." She looks over her shoulder. "Tell them I can't come right now. I'm not leaving her."

Another doctor I don't recognize walks in, a blue line of scrubs broken by a pale face. "Mrs. Harris, have you ever experienced this before?"

"I don't know, I don't think so."

"Is there anything you do when this happens?"

I don't understand. "My heart races when I'm anxious, but I wasn't nervous until people started coming in to check my heart."

"Right, no problem." He leaves.

"Do you want some ice?" I never say no to Anika, as many times as she asks and puts the plastic spoon to my lips.

"I'm so scared," I say again. I'm alive as long as I'm speaking. Anika moves closer. "Tell me about your kids."

"The oldest, Eliot, is a girl," I say. "And she's beautiful." I need her to know that. The one who is so responsible that she can fly under the radar. I need her to know she's been noticed, loved. Not forgotten. "The next is Christopher, we call him Tophs." I'm too anxious to spell it out. "And the youngest is Juliet." Finally, a Harris child with a name I don't have to explain. Anika will let them know their mother remembered, spoke their names.

I can hear someone at my feet, just beyond the corner, "A thirty-seven-year-old . . ." and then words I can't make out. "Who is caring for her?" another asks. I don't remember the exact response, but what I process is that no one has claimed me. I am alone; the surgeons are in clinic with new patients, and no one in the hospital knows what to do with me.

After thirty minutes or two hours or who knows, another face appears at my side: My chest X-ray is clear, and Cardiology isn't concerned about my EKG. There is one theory: at the end of the operation, the plastic surgeon put nitroglycerin paste on my chest, which can help traumatized skin but also dilates blood vessels. It probably caused my blood pressure to drop, then my heart to race to try and keep up. Someone would ask him about scraping the paste off.

Hope breaks through. If the medicine is just doing its job on my blood vessels, which don't need dilating . . . If someone could unzip the white surgical bra, cut through the plastic saran wrap below, and rub off the excess paste, then my heart would slow down.

"Let me see," Anika says. "I bet if we can get your husband

back here, your heart rate will go down." *Yes, that's good, he's the one.* She's on the phone, speaking deftly in code, giving him an indirect way into this restricted space that I cannot leave and he cannot enter. She refuses to break for lunch until Paul arrives.

"Yep, there it goes," she says, looking at the monitor as Paul comes close. "Down by twenty."

Paul sets down a black plastic bag of Mr. Pibb bottles. "She had me driving all around town," he jokes with Anika. Turns out he'd finally found a little market on a side street with vending machines out front. Paul finds a way. I feel silly for asking him to bring something that kept him away. I'd made the request in the Before. I'll later learn he had no idea there'd been a problem. His earlier updates from the surgeons were enthusiastic. It wasn't until Anika's second call that he discerned the need to rush back.

I feel good with him here, good that my pulse is finally down from the 150s, and I remember something Anika told me. "She likes grape Crush," I tell Paul. If I get out of here, I'll bring her a cart full of two-liters.

Paul sits down to my right and holds my hand. His bare hand, and I have never been more certain that even if he can't save me, he absolutely cannot leave me.

I only wish I couldn't read his face above the mask. "Is that her heart rate?" he asks, looking at the monitors.

"Sorta," Anika answers, trailing off. She knows my disposition by now, probably doesn't want to lie but doesn't want me to read Paul's surprise. Being flat on my back without my glasses or contacts has protected me from seeing any scary vitals for myself. Everything I've gathered is from what I've heard.

Another doctor parts the curtain: "See, your pulse jumped up as soon as I walked in," as though this is a game of Gotcha! I've organized. There's some talk about getting me to pee, and even though on road trips I can pee through the eye of a needle into coffee cups, old shoes, and plastic hamster balls, you name it, I cannot make myself pee onto this grown folks' diaper Anika has situated around me. It's just her, Paul, and me, and my urine has dammed itself inside, trying to protect my dignity.

"Do you want to try a catheter?" she asks.

My eyes open wide. "Yes!" Next to babies, catheters are the best part of childbirth.

"Well, why didn't you just say so?"

Being catheterized is great, but have you ever found a Black woman who will go to bat for you? A young resident walks in after I've been in recovery for about three hours and asks to take a look at the site. I'm used to this by now. Everyone politely asks, unzips me, studies what I'm afraid to see, nods, and zips me back up. And I'm always rooting for a brother in medicine, but this guy does nothing to ease my distress.

"What about the nitro paste?" Paul asks. "They mentioned scraping it off?"

"Well, it should start wearing off after several hours, so I'm not sure about taking it off."

My eyes burn. I'm stuck. The thing that's hurting me has to stay on me? "What about something for anxiety?" I ask.

"We don't like to give those medications on the first day of surgery, because it can mask other serious underlying issues."

Hot tears slide from the sides of my eyes. Fear pulls back the steely cover every time.

"Look at her," Paul says to him.

Anika stands there, and just from her posture, I know her lips are thin and tight underneath.

"Is there anything else I can do for you?" This man is an actual robot. I want his head to explode, wires popping out like on the cartoons. I want having a Black doctor to mean I'll be well cared for. I'm angry, half-heartbroken it doesn't.

But as soon as he leaves, Anika finds a way. Within minutes, I have medicine through my IV. This is smart, empathic healthcare.

After four or five hours, my heart rate down and blood pressure stable, I'm ready to leave recovery for my overnight room. A doctor whose shape and face I've come to recognize peeks in one last time. "I don't have many, but you gave me all the gray hairs on my head," he says.

What if the preventive surgery had been a danger greater than the risk of breast cancer? Was it worth it? What do you do when the fear and risk and percentages are all rational, all real?

Back when I was praying about becoming Paul's girlfriend, I experienced a millennial girl's equivalent of a burning-bush moment. A fiery female preacher called to me from a small crowd, said there were two questions I'd been asking God, and the answer to both was yes. I could never settle on the second question, but I knew the question I cared about more than anything. I went straight back to my apartment that night to tell Paul we were on. Thankfully, he hadn't given up on me. I mean, don't get me wrong, I was cute and worth all that wait and more, but still. We haven't been apart since.

I prayed and fasted about the decision to have a mastectomy too. Though not for forty days as I'd done in college before our engagement. Fasting with kids isn't pretty past day three. The kids are like, "Mommy?!" And I'm all, "Depart from me!" While fasting, I envisioned myself being cared for in a hospital room. The idea that God might want to love me this way, a way that didn't put science and faith at odds, stayed with me. And the fact that my breast surgeon was a boss lady with impeccable style didn't hurt. She'd walk into appointments wearing my same color combination, only her blue shoes were pointed heels, not canvas slip-ons with coffee stains, and her magenta top was a beautiful sleeveless blouse, not a crumpled tee from the Loft. She was a fashion icon with a scalpel and a mother's touch.

The third piece of the decision came through the words of author Elizabeth Wurtzel. When she died from breast cancer in January 2020, I found and read her essay for *The New York Times*, "The Breast Cancer Gene and Me," published in 2015. "I have waiting rooms in my future, full of *Golf Digest* and *Time* from four months ago and that same issue of *W* that's always there," she wrote. "I have waiting ahead. If you don't like waiting, cancer is not for you." These lines haunted me most.

January was typically a scan month, when I was injected with dye, either for a mammogram or MRI with contrast. I knew the waiting routine well—plastic-wrapped crackers and a Keurig, women my age and older in robes, and that was without a cancer diagnosis. Wurtzel's mention of the old *Golf Digest*, of the worst part not being the pain or the big, scary prognosis, unnerved me. There were mundane, boring parts of cancer. I couldn't forget that. I told my breast surgeon I was finally ready to schedule my prophylactic mastectomy. After all this time, I chose the year of a pandemic to have elective surgery. TAR. My April surgery date was pushed back to August.

Between April and August, grief and rage gripped my family,

maybe the world, like never before. The global pandemic did not stop, did not care about these other traumas, the way they layered in under its watch. Neither did the White House, neither did UVA, an institution I knew wasn't perfect or equitable yet I had loved. Murders of unarmed Black people made headlines, and the righteously angry spilled out onto the streets in masks, demanding justice for George Floyd, Breonna Taylor, Ahmaud Arbery, Elijah McClain, and others. My boy seized at dawn for the third time, which left me walking around the house filling water bottles, washing clothes, clipping fingernails, anything to recuse myself from thought. My husband's denial of tenure by the University of Virginia gained national attention, and, while his dean and the committee never apologized, their decision was reversed, and I quickly spiraled from glee and relief to depression, because betrayal, even by white people, is betrayal. Days later, a surgeon removed all my breast tissue and I awoke sideways and sweaty, a watch dripping time down a tree branch. When the nurse came to tell Paul visiting hours were over that night, he politely but firmly said, "I'm not leaving her," and she returned with a pillow. He slept straight up in a chair next to my bed wearing a mask all night.

*A lot of things are wrong.*

*A lot of things have happened to me.*

*What if I told you we were falling together?*


After I'm discharged the next day, friends, neighbors, church members, and Paul's colleagues spoil us with Thai food, lattes, pizza, and ice cream. A friend brings half gallons all the way from the Penn State Creamery, and on a night when I can't sleep, when the painkillers have worn off and my head jerks me awake in terror every time I doze, I keep vigil over my strange, stitched up body with a carton of banana ice cream and a cold spoon. There is a word used for people in my position: *previvor.* You are no longer naïve, unaware of your genetic history; neither are you waiting in the strange middle space, wondering if you should act before cancer has a chance to act upon you. My body doesn't feel like mine, my mind even less so, and with drains hanging at my sides from the incision sites, it's hard to imagine I've escaped or preempted anything. Yet I have crossed over, to another space, where I'm far from healed but free from the looming question, the "What should I do?" that I held on to for four years. That is not nothing.

I don't tell the kids details of my surgery, and I hide my drains under a special A-line mastectomy robe. One day we'll talk more—I'll be a wide-open book, an internet search, a sketcher of Punnett squares, a smoother of curls and kisser of cheeks. I'll be whatever they need me to be.

For now, they know Mommy is fragile, and they fall into mini-caretaking roles that fit their distinct personalities. Tophs shuts his eyes in bed and prays God will keep me safe. Eliot brings me a chest pillow and ginger ale on the couch, reminding her younger siblings to "Watch out for Mommy!" At four, Juliet reminds me so much of myself, a lifetime of facial expressions, without the acquired fear of vulnerability. One night she pulls my face in close to hers at bedtime, kisses my lips, and says, "I'm so glad there's not a way to un-mom."

Tell me, then, after all the searching, what is left to know.

———

*This moment isn't a dream, and yet it moves like one, sharp in some places, blurred at its edges, persistent in the way it finds me.*

*My family has gathered in the Outer Banks again, and I'm sitting poolside in a white plastic chair. A black hose feeds water into the small pool, filled with brown children breaking its too-blue surface with their hand-standed legs, and flailing, freestyle arms. Their skin like glazed pecans, shimmering copper, and toasted marshmallow. Three belong to Paul and me, the other two are my sisters'.*

*Paul holds Juliet in her pink swim cap and purple ruffled one-piece as she begs him to let her go, certain she can swim. Her head dips below the surface for a moment and she returns sputtering and lays her head on his broad shoulder. Not yet, baby.*

*Eliot, ever cautious and proud, practices pushing off and gliding from one edge of the pool to another, a distance of five or six feet. She's beaming when her face lifts from the water, and even though I've watched her ten times now, I give her another thumbs-up. This is a big deal, baby.*

*My niece Mynne follows behind Eliot, both in stroke and years, having found a reliable big sister who is happy to lead. She scorns her cousin McClain for spraying them with the hose by pressing his thumb over the hole.*

*After abandoning a unicorn floaty more trouble than it's worth, Tophs has settled into a nook in the shallow end where the pool curves out and back in. He can stand there in his wetsuit, the sleeves stretched to his elbows, neon goggles spreading his eyes apart, frog-like.*

*He's learning to swim this summer, coached by a high school student back home. But more than anything, he likes to be underwater. Movement across the water, end to end, is not his goal. Instead, he plugs his nose with his right hand and slips beneath. He likes seeing things underwater, he's told us.*

*He sinks down to the bottom, as though taking a seat for morning circle, then allows his body to float three feet up, the back of his navy wetsuit rising to the top, before he stands up for air. He wipes his face, flicking off the wet, before grabbing his nose and sliding back down. Air is a necessary inconvenience. He does not gasp for it. He rises, receives it, returns beneath.*

*Are you okay, baby?*

*He places the back of his head just under the hose, where his tight and low curls break the steady river of water into dozens of tiny streams.*

*Then he's in pike position, disappearing without a sound. And as his sister and cousin call his name and ask him to watch their tricks, he comes up for air, then slips below, never even looking their way. They turn angry, and I know he should answer them, but he's hit a stride. He should live this moment without bother.*

*"Mommy, when I was underwater, I was sitting crisscross applesauce on the floor."*

*He, it turns out, was always there. Seeing things the way he was made to see.*

*And who was I? Not his life raft, not his anchor, not the hand that let him fall. All along, in and out of knowing, in every space between, I was his mother.*

# ACKNOWLEDGMENTS

Julie Buntin is not only my brilliant editor. She has crafted herself a cozy nook in my heart, and I will never let her leave. Generous, intuitive, and whip-smart, she never gave up on what she knew this book could be. Julie, thank you for making it easy to trust you and be known by you. I will stop sending you videos of Tophs the day you turn eighty-three.

This book is not this book without Nicole Chung, a fierce and gracious writer, editor, and friend. We met in the bathroom, and I've never felt so grateful for a finicky bladder. Nicole never stops championing other writers, especially those traditionally marginalized, and she holds her friends close, even when it means sharing their grief.

Whenever I talk to my agent, Bridget Matzie, I momentarily believe I can take over the world. Got a problem? Bridget has three solutions. She offers me a perfectly titrated mix of confidence and wisdom, without one drop of arrogance.

Nicole Caputo, who I've concluded is made of stars and peonies and clouds, designed this gorgeous cover, and I hope she never forgets what a gift she's given me.

Thank you to the all-star team at Catapult including: Jonathan Lee, Alicia Kroell (whom I emailed daily and on Saturdays twice), Megan Fishmann, Rachel Fershleiser, Laura Gonzalez, Jordan Koluch, Wah-Ming Chang, Dustin Kurtz, Katie Boland, and Laura Berry. Thanks to Sue Ducharme too.

Some fabulous writers endorsed this book early on. They make me want to be a more generous human. Thank you to Nicole Chung, Meaghan O'Connell, Porochista Khakpour, Deesha Philyaw, and Heather Lanier.

Shannon O'Neill has been a loyal guide and friend since my first night of grad school. Thank you to everyone from Hopkins who made me better: Cathy Alter, Elyse Moody, Marina Koestler Ruben, Mimi Kirk, Rebecca Sinderbrand, Matt Pusateri, Rhea Kennedy Morgenstern, Halima Aziza Jenkins, Jean Doan, and Lauren Hassani.

A high-five and fist bump to those who've cared for Tophs, including: Dr. Quillian, Shelley, Dr. Peroutka, Dr. Humberson, Paige, Laila, Jillian, Rosser, Anita, Dr. Evie, Dr. Marcus Potter, Maëlys, Laura, Stephanie, Ida, Tracy, Renee, Emily K., Kristin, Dr. Fowler, and many more.

Big hugs to my C'ville people, who kept me afloat with lattes, scripture, ice cream, and princess cake. Trying to name you all is like catching cicadas with a sock, but here goes: Leigh, Cam, Kristen, Taison, Andrea, Judge Lisa, Lisa W., Naomi, Jess, Randi, Ellen,

Espo, Joanne, Thiede, Tiffany, Lapp, Mia, Jillian, Shelby, Erica, Kate, Ashlee, Frankie, Blaire, Jaime, Barb, Lori, Dana, Karen, Christy, and Dodd. Thanks to Jerry, who brought Paul an almond milk steamer after Tophs's seizure. And much love to the irreplaceable baristas at Shenandoah Joe who know our drink orders by heart.

I love and miss our Victory Church family. Thanks to Christine Hoover, Fran Hartwig, and Cynthia Fuller, who made being a pastor's wife seem possible. Thanks to Charlene Brown for always being down for church/life/Twizzler chats.

Erin Maupin started as a mom friend and became my third sister. Thanks for the dresses, the conversations, the pastries, the being there.

Shamika, thank you for letting me text you pictures of seven-layer cakes. One day we will eat all the glory.

John Warner and Chris Monk of McSweeney's believed in me when I only believed in mastitis. Hugs to Michelle Mirsky, whose column and friendship set the bar high.

Ms. Hall, my first grade teacher, let me write in my journal for an extended time whenever I wanted. Thank you for seeing me.

I'm grateful for Mick, Steph, Melody, and Daisy, who tricked me into believing UVA was an HBCU. Well played, cool Black kids. Thanks to Mimi and Melissa, who helped me get through the non-academic parts of college.

My friend Barrie hasn't stopped caring for me since our days as green teaching assistants at UVA. Thank you to Grace Hale, who blew open my thinking in the American Studies program. Professors Dylan Penningroth, Deborah McDowell, and M. Rick Turner greatly supported and challenged me. And the Endowed Professors crew has always had my back.

Micah, Jasmine, Bianca, and Tyler—if y'all don't take over the world, I want my money back.

Interning with NPR's *Tell Me More* with Michel Martin remains a highlight of my life. Teshima, just like you advised, I stayed on my mission.

I am delighted to know Jocelyn Johnson, who has nurtured my kids with her art and the world with her words. *My Monticello* is the just the beginning.

Cathryne Keller is a sharp and kind editor. She should be a billionaire. Meaghan O'Connell is a terrific editor and hilarious person, but she'd be fine with a cool million. Jen Gann is an editor and friend I would trust to care for my children, as well as my words.

Thanks to Yetunde Oyeneyin for getting me out of the saddle with that Tamia remix and leading me through the pandemic with a space that honored and centered Blackness.

I've had terrific doctors, nurses, and therapists in my thirty-eight years, including Dr. Dawdy and Rachel. Thanks to Jason, who told me the book didn't have to be perfect; it had to be true. Thank you, Tim, for making our family stronger. I'm beyond grateful for Dr. Yost, a dream therapist. I do not prefer surgery, but Dr. Showalter is a boss-mom-surgeon with impeccable style. Anika, thank you for never leaving my side.

Lindsay Avner has remained a call away, helping me process tough news and prepare for surgery. She's been a source of encouragement, a friend when she didn't have to be.

I'm thankful for my first friend ever, Simone Gabel. And Kelcye Ball, who has been a bright and stylish light in my life since high school.

May the memory of those we lost so quickly be a blessing:

JoAnn LaMuth, Bennett Charles McClurkin-Gibney (the original Brony), Teshima Walker, and David Everett. I like to imagine handing a copy of the book to David, my favorite writing instructor. Maybe he'd tear up a little, and I'd sidestep the moment of vulnerability by making fun of his graying hair.

Kaitlyn, thank you for the watermelons and pumpkins, but mostly for being open to sitting with questions we can't answer. I'm so proud of you. Keep going.

I don't know why my best friend, Remington, has stuck with me since college, but I'm so grateful. Rem, you are a true boo who saves the day in fashionable flats.

When I am standing next to my big sisters, no one can tell me anything. Not one thing. Autumn and Sienna, thank you for ensuring I've always had what I needed—whether a NUK pacifier, money for school, a case of Red Vines, or a text thread about busted slippers and panties people think will sell online. I love you forever.

Thanks to my stepdad, Bryan, for all the Cokes, tennis texts, and love. Mom, thank you for reminding me I am not only made of fear. You told me I was creative and smart and tenacious. You taught me to read and fly kites, to give quickly and freely. Dad, thanks for that Bible and so much more. No one else understands my need to scour the earth for the best ice cream quite like you (and Grandma). You're so easy to talk to. Grandma Betty, you are the GOAT, and not the kind you pet, though I do like giving you hugs. I love you all, and I hope I made you proud.

Eliot, Tophs, and Juliet: You are shiny, brilliant, hilarious gifts. Here are two more things I know to be true: 1) You are so loved, and 2) You are never alone. Thank you for letting me be Mommy.

And to Paul, whose touch still sends a good shock through my body, whose arms, now more than ever, feel like home. You and I are more than this boy we made, but I'm so glad he and his sisters belong to us. You and I are made of trolleys and grilled cheese, of rose petals and prayers, of anger and renewal, of love and of dust. There is no one I'd rather start and end my days with, start and end my adult life with. I love you.

© Eze Arros

TAYLOR HARRIS is a writer, wife, and mom
of three who lives in Charlottesville, Virginia. Her
work has appeared in *O Quarterly*, *The Washington Post*, *Longreads*, *The Cut*, *Romper*, *Parents*,
*McSweeney's*, and other publications.